Journalism: A Very Short Introduction

VERY SHORT INTRODUCTIONS are for anyone wanting a stimulating and accessible way in to a new subject. They are written by experts, and have been published in more than 25 languages worldwide.

The series began in 1995, and now represents a wide variety of topics in history, philosophy, religion, science, and the humanities. Over the next few years it will grow to a library of around 200 volumes – a Very Short Introduction to everything from ancient Egypt and Indian philosophy to conceptual art and cosmology.

Very Short Introductions available now:

Available soon:

For more information visit our web site

Ian Hargreaves

JOURNALISM

A Very Short Introduction

OXFORD
UNIVERSITY PRESS

OXFORD

UNIVERSITY PRESS

Great Clarendon Street, Oxford OX2 6DP

Oxford University Press is a department of the University of Oxford.
It furthers the University's objective of excellence in research, scholarship,
and education by publishing worldwide in

Oxford New York

Auckland Cape Town Dar es Salaam Hong Kong Karachi
Kuala Lumpur Madrid Melbourne Mexico City Nairobi
New Delhi Shanghai Taipei Toronto

With offices in

Argentina Austria Brazil Chile Czech Republic France Greece
Guatemala Hungary Italy Japan Poland Portugal Singapore
South Korea Switzerland Thailand Turkey Ukraine Vietnam

Oxford is a registered trade mark of Oxford University Press
in the UK and in certain other countries

Published in the United States
by Oxford University Press Inc., New York

© Ian Hargreaves 2003, 2005

The moral rights of the author have been asserted

Database right Oxford University Press (maker)

First published as Journalism: Truth or Dare, 2003
First published as a Very Short Introduction 2005

British Library Cataloguing in Publication Data

Data available

Library of Congress Cataloging in Publication Data

Data available

ISBN 0-19-280656-4 978-0-19-280656-7

1 3 5 7 9 10 8 6 4 2

Typeset by RefineCatch Ltd, Bungay, Suffolk
Printed in Great Britain by
TJ International Ltd., Padstow, Cornwall

Contents

To Ben, Kelda, Yoko, Zola, and Adele

Acknowledgements

Countless people have contributed to the thinking in these pages, especially my fellow-journalists at the *Keighley News*, the *Bradford Telegraph and Argus*, the *Financial Times*, the BBC, the *Independent*, and the *New Statesman*, my main places of work in the last thirty years.

The motivation for the book, however, arose during my years at the Centre for Journalism Studies at Cardiff University, working alongside Professor John Hartley. Professional journalists, especially British ones, are given to disdain for the work of media scholars like Hartley; but my time in Cardiff convinced me that journalists would do a better job for the citizens they presume to serve if they encouraged more critical interrogation of the way journalism works. This slim volume aims to support such interrogation.

Roch, Pembrokeshire

May 2005

List of illustrations

Introduction
The paradox of power

Journalism entered the twenty-first century caught in a paradox of its own making. We have more news and more influential journalism, across an unprecedented range of media, than at any time since the birth of the free press in the eighteenth century. Yet journalism is also under unprecedented attack, from politicians, philosophers, the general public, anti-globalization radicals, religious groups and even from journalists themselves. This book is an attempt to explain this paradox and to explore the possible implications.

The first stage of the paradox, the ascent in journalism's influence, is easily explained. Its underlying cause is the growth in the cultural, political, and economic value of information, facilitated by the emergence of new, cheap electronic technologies to distribute and display news and the industry of commentary which today surrounds the news. It is now widely understood that without abundant and accessible information we can have neither the democracy in which we believe nor the economic growth and consumer choice we desire.

News, which was once difficult and expensive to obtain, today surrounds us like the air we breathe. Much of it is literally ambient: displayed on computers, public billboards, trains, aircraft, and mobile phones. Where once news had to be sought out in expensive and scarce news sheets, today it is ubiquitous and very largely free at the point of consumption. Satisfying news hunger no longer involves a twice daily diet of a morning newspaper and evening TV news bulletin: news comes in snack-form, to be grazed, and at every level of quality; even to be programmed to order, to arrive, pre-sorted, via your personal digital assistant. Where once journalism's reach was confined by the time it took to haul bundles of newsprint from one end of a country to the other, now it is global, instantaneous, and interactive.

But there are problems with this new culture of news. Because there is so much of it, we find it difficult to sort the good from the bad. The fact that it is mostly obtainable without direct payment may mean that we value it less. As a generation grows up unaccustomed to the idea that news costs money, the economics of resource-intensive journalism, like in-depth investigations, are undermined.

Junk journalism

Also, when information travels as fast as it does today, it can wreak destruction before there is time for it to be understood. In the world of instant journalism, reputations are destroyed and privacies trivially invaded in the time it takes to switch TV channels. Junk food may be convenient and taste OK at the first bite, but its popularity raises longer term questions of public health. So too with junk journalism. Today's television journalists shoot pictures in desert war-zones and beam them via satellite for transmission around the world. These stories get most prominence if the shots are visually exciting: violence is desirable, death a bonus. Better still if the journalist is young, glamorous, and famous. Less melodramatic, but more important stories, about education, health, diplomacy and community relations, get less coverage. Meanwhile financial journalists are hard-wired to market information systems to deliver instant appraisal which moves prices, raising temptations of personal financial gain and underplaying longer run, more significant economic and business issues. The circumstances of modern news thus test the journalist's judgement and honesty, not in fundamentally new ways, but more routinely and at greater speed than ever before. If the journalist is secretly the tool of some invisible public relations machine or vested commercial interest, it is the public whose interest is betrayed.

In politics, democracy itself is at stake in this world of high-speed, always-on news. Political reporters pronounce sudden verdicts upon the politicians they often outshine in fame and, as a result, parliaments everywhere feel themselves reduced to side-attractions in the great non-stop media show. In 1828, the British historian Macaulay dubbed the press gallery in Parliament a 'fourth estate' of the realm. Today, the news media appear to have become the first estate, able to topple monarchs and turn Parliament into a talking shop which ceases to exist if journalists turn their backs. Television interviewers wag their fingers at government ministers, called to account in the headmaster's studio, live, before a mass audience. Since more people vote in reality television shows than in elections for the European Parliament or municipal authorities, the response of politicians has been to try, desperately, to be more like television: conversational, friendly, emotional, and not too demanding. How else can Congressmen and parliamentarians retain the interest of the young? How else to be heard through the cacophony of information overload?

The crisis of trust

There are many symptoms of the difficulties now piling up around this pervasive journalism. We know, from opinion surveys, that journalists are less trusted and less esteemed than used to be the case. In terms of trust, journalists rank alongside the politicians they have helped drag down, but behind business executives and civil servants and way behind the most respected professionals such as doctors, teachers, and scientists. 'The future for the press in the new millennium looks bleak,' says Dr Carl Jensen, founder of

3

Project Censored, which has been tracking press issues in the US for twenty-five years.

> 'The press has the power to stimulate people to clean up the environment, prevent nuclear proliferation, force crooked politicians out of office, reduce poverty, provide quality health care for all people and even to save the lives of millions of people as it did in Ethiopia in 1984. But instead, we are using it to promote sex, violence, and sensationalism and to line the pockets of already wealthy media moguls.'

Jensen's view was widely echoed in the United States during the scandal that engulfed President Bill Clinton over his sexual misbehaviour with the White House intern Monica Lewinsky. The American news media, including some of its most highly reputed newspapers and broadcasters, were widely judged to be peddling gossip, rumour, and unchecked facts as they scrambled to outdo each other for sensation and scoops. Critics saw this as part of a pattern, evident in coverage of an earlier celebrity scandal, the O. J. Simpson trial, when the news media were accused of caring too much about soap opera and too little about justice. The public's reaction to President Clinton's 'Zippergate' was to turn against the news media, rather than the president. The very fact that journalists all over the world so casually add the suffix 'gate' to any potential scandal, however trivial, itself indicates a certain loss of seriousness since the days of Watergate, which hangs as a long shadow over the endeavours of investigative journalists. More recently, American journalism has been buffeted by a series of internal scandals involving faked reports within some of the country's most esteemed news organizations. One of these led to the resignation of the two most senior editors of the New York Times.

Concerned journalists fight back

Through events like these, scepticism about journalism has started to eat at the soul of American democratic values. According to a

1999 poll, 53 per cent of Americans, reared on a First Amendment to the Constitution that forbids any curtailment of the right to free expression of individuals or newspapers, had reached the conclusion that the press has too much freedom. At the same time, a movement of 'concerned journalists' has emerged, advocating a return to basic professional standards of accurate and balanced reporting and campaigning against what it sees as an over-commercial news media. The new media owners, say the concerned journalists, are deflecting journalism from its sacred mission to inform citizens without fear and favour, pandering instead to the appetites of shareholders for quarter-on-quarter profits growth. 'We are facing the possibility that independent news will be replaced by self-interested commercialism posing as news,' say the authors of one of the movement's manifestos. They continue:

> 'The First Amendment – that a free press is an independent institution – is threatened for the first time in our history without government meddling. In this world, the First Amendment becomes a property right establishing ground rules for free economic competition, not free speech. This is a fundamental and epic change with enormous implications for democratic society.'

A similar story can be heard, in one form or another, all over the democratic world, though its intensity ebbs and flows. In Italy, the Prime Minister, Silvio Berlusconi, is regarded by his critics as commanding patronage in the state broadcasting system, RAI, as well as still benefiting from his history as a dominant figure in Italy's largest commercial television group, Mediaset. In effect, say his critics, Berlusconi pulls the strings in 90 per cent of the country's television journalism which is, as a result, fatally compromised. Vaclav Havel, President of the Czech Republic and veteran of one of post Cold War Europe's most passionate fights for free media, chose World Press Freedom Day in 2002 to issue this warning: 'In a situation where there will be no direct political oppression and censorship,' he said, 'there might be more complex issues, especially at the economic level, that may affect freedom of speech. Italy might represent an early form of this problem.'

In Britain, the agenda of concern focuses upon the powerful position of the Australian–American Rupert Murdoch, who controls over a third of the national newspaper market and owns the country's dominant pay television platform. Murdoch is regarded by many as an outsider capable of making or breaking governments. At the same time, there is persistent anxiety about lax standards in the press generally. A defining moment here was the violent death of Princess Diana in a Parisian subway in August 1997, her car chased by freelance photographers employed by British (and other) newspaper photographers. At the Princess's funeral, her brother accused publishers of having 'blood on their hands'. Throughout the 1990s, the Press Complaints Commission, a self-regulatory body that oversees with debatable effectiveness an editor's code of ethics, struggled to update its rules to meet public and political pressure. The PCC's reputation was not helped when, in 2002, its chairman, Lord Wakeham, a former minister in the government of Margaret Thatcher, turned out to be a director of Enron, the American energy company that cooked its books. Wakeham was forced to step down from the PCC, to be replaced by the retiring ambassador to Washington, Sir Christopher Meyer, another establishment figure charged with the task of burnishing the press's troubled image.

A new challenge to press freedom

It was in this atmosphere that the philosopher Dr Onora O'Neill delivered the 2002 Reith Lectures, a prestigious series named in honour of the first director general of the BBC. She argued that the classic eighteenth-century doctrine of press freedom had outlived its usefulness; that it belonged to a more heroic time. In modern democracies, press freedom was being used as a cloak to shield media conglomerates' domination of public discussion 'in which misinformation may be peddled uncorrected and in which reputations may be selectively shredded or magnified. A free press is not an unconditional good.' When the media mislead, she added, 'the wells of public discourse and public life are poisoned'.

Meanwhile those with a closer and more venal relationship with journalism have long dribbled petrol into this flame of criticism. Alan Clark, a colourful British Conservative Member of Parliament, in an essay written just before his death, dismissed journalists as: 'fellows with, in the main, squalid and unfulfilling private lives, insecure in their careers, and suffering a considerable degree of dependence on alcohol and narcotics.' This comment echoes the words of Conrad (Lord) Black, a substantial Canadian publisher who accumulated press interests in Britain, North America, and Israel, while characterizing journalists as 'ignorant, lazy, opinionated, intellectually dishonest, and inadequately supervised'. That was before Black found himself in trouble with the law for an alleged fraud against his company's shareholders.

A still more searching version of the moral case against journalistic practice has been made by Janet Malcolm in her study of a dispute between a convicted murderer and a journalist who wrote an account of the criminal's life. This is how Malcolm drum-rolls her central argument at the opening of her essay:

'Every journalist who is not too stupid or full of himself to notice what is going on knows that what he does is morally indefensible. He is a kind of confidence man, preying upon people's vanity, ignorance or loneliness, gaining their trust and betraying them without remorse ... Journalists justify their treachery in various ways according to their temperaments. The more pompous talk about freedom of speech and "the public's right to know"; the least talented talk about Art; the seemliest murmur about earning a living.'

Anyone who has worked for a long time in journalism and thought about what they are doing will recognize that there is some force in these characterizations. It is easy for journalism to be morally casual, even as it makes large moral claims for itself. So when journalism is accused by those it serves of privileging sensation before significance, celebrity before achievement, intrusion before purposeful investigation and entertainment before reliability, the charge demands a response. Journalism stands accused of being not so much a public service as a public health hazard.

The end of journalism?

The response of journalists to these accusations is anything but uniform. Many journalists will (mostly quietly) admit to sharing the anxieties of the 'concerned journalists' of the United States. They can see that greater concentration of corporate ownership of the news media is cutting newsroom budgets and undermining journalistic integrity, giving advertisers and sponsors unwarranted influence over news agendas. 'Too many once-distinguished news organisations have lost their lustre; too few new ones have materialized,' say two senior editors from the *Washington Post*. Their book, lest you should miss the point, is subtitled: *American Journalism in Peril*. Journalists also worry about the riks that new media technologies are turning them into 'robo-hacks,' prefiguring, according to one commentator, 'the end of journalism'. There is concern about the polarization of the news media with, at one end, badly paid and sometimes inadequately trained young people in smaller newspapers, radio stations, magazines and on-line news services and, at the other, a handful of celebrity journalists who present television shows or write famous newspaper columns and earn show business salaries.

The late Paul Foot, a distinguished journalistic sleuth, has lamented the death of investigative journalism and John Pilger, the campaigning Australian journalist, has complained at the ease with which most journalists are duped into following the 'hidden agenda' of political or business power. Other journalists express alarm at the casual blood-thirstiness of modern journalism towards elected politicians; the trend, in Adam Gopnik's words, from dining with presidents to dining on them. As John Lloyd, a writer for the *Financial Times*, has said: the famous dictum of Harold Evans, who edited the London *Sunday Times* in the 1970s, that the journalist interviewing a politician should always ask 'why is this bastard lying to me?' has 'passed from radical fearlessness to a commercial strategy with big implications for the health of our public life'. Lloyd calls for new mechanisms to 'interrogate the interrogators.'

Crisis, what crisis?

There is, however, a second and more widespread journalistic response to this attack on the professional standards of journalism. It asks, with a world-weary expression: 'crisis, what crisis?' Journalists, these people say, have always been under attack: the more ferocious the attack, the healthier journalism must be. Janet Malcolm's confidence trickster is a necessary agent of society's ability to examine and purge itself; the increasing sophistication of governments and corporations demands more journalistic ferocity, not less. There is, in this view, no case for agitation about the way that journalists frame their ethical codes, get trained and are regulated.

This inside-the-profession insouciance has a long history in journalism. Nicolas Tomalin, a star reporter for the *Sunday Times*, who was killed in the Yom Kippur War in 1973, advised aspiring reporters that 'the only qualities essential for real success in journalism are ratlike cunning, a plausible manner and a little literary ability'. H. L. Mencken, the great Baltimore iconoclast, considered journalism 'a craft to be mastered in four days and abandoned at the first sign of a better job'. No inflated comparisons here between journalists, doctors, scientists, and lawyers.

Behind Mencken's irony lies a serious point. Journalism, he says, cannot be likened to professions such as medicine and the law because the journalist 'is unable, as yet, to control admission to his craft'. Indeed, the only societies where admission to the practice of journalism is controlled are those that have abandoned or never known democracy, such as the Soviet Union in the cold war period, or numerous countries in Africa, the Middle East, and Asia. The requirement to belong to a state-endorsed 'union of journalists' or 'press club' guarantees that real journalism, if it exists at all, will take place by subterfuge. The core democratic right to free expression gives, in principle, every citizen the right to be a journalist, to report a fact, and to publish an opinion. Journalism, by this line of reasoning, is philosophically and practically beyond regulation by any body associated with the state. Even to place a heavy emphasis upon training or professional standards can diminish this necessary freedom: just as free expression guarantees tolerance for pornography and bad novels, so too, it must avert its eyes from bad journalism. The alternative turns journalism into another branch of established power.

Hyper-journalism

Yet there is something too evasive in this script for our own times, when the mass media exercise global, corporate power on an unprecedented scale. Journalism today reflects not so much the motivations of clamorous individual citizens, at risk of exploitation by big corporations or mighty governments, as the motivations of vast and often highly profitable media institutions. To do its job in a modern society, journalism needs the capital such organizations provide, but with that power comes a new requirement from civil society to balance the power and responsibility of this global hyper-journalism.

Journalists need to be reminded that it is only through democratic civil society that they have secured and maintained the 'free press' privileges upon which their effectiveness depends. In return, the public has a right to expect that journalists will take seriously the responsibilities that come with their privileges. Journalists are not lone rangers with a pocket full of silver bullets; they are individuals operating within an understood economic, cultural, and political framework. That is why, in my view, journalists should welcome the new mood of interrogation about their values, standards, and professional practices, whilst robustly defending free journalism's importance in the functioning of any open society.

New technology, new politics

There is another, important sense in which the framework of discussion assumed by a Mencken or a Tomalin is anachronistic. Both writers were making their argument with reference, essentially, to newspaper journalism. Today, newspapers are in remorseless, if gradual, decline. American research reports that, today, a minority of people say that they read a newspaper the previous day, compared with 58 per cent only a decade ago. In Britain, more than a quarter of people today do not regard newspapers as an important source of news, whereas almost everyone watches television news. This change is of huge significance, not least because of the difference in political and economic culture which attended the birth of the press and the electronic media. Newspapers have their roots in commercial markets and a period when citizens were struggling, via their newspapers, for democratic rights. By contrast, radio was born on the threshold of a totalitarian era in Europe and, for technical reasons, developed initially either as a state monopoly or an oligopoly licensed by the state, based upon the state's ownership of broadcast spectrum. Television, which came to maturity in the second half of the twentieth century, also involved very strong state influence, either through licensing, in democracies, or direct control in more authoritarian settings. As General de Gaulle, the French president, once remarked: 'My enemies have the press, so I keep television.' De Gaulle's successors have, like their peers in other European countries, presided over a significant loosening of monopoly, but no one doubts the influence the French government still exerts in television, through its appointments to the country's regulatory system and by other, less obvious, means. Television, in most parts of the world, remains a heavily regulated industry, especially with regard to its news services, although this control is now being challenged by digital television, which delivers hundreds of channels via satellite and terrestrial transmission systems.

In this third, digital era of electronic news media, based around the internet and other broadband communications technologies, the formative creative and political cultures are different again, this time based upon a fusion of economic liberalism and globalization with a technology rooted partly in the Pentagon and partly in the world's leading research universities. It is hard to say whether the political culture of the internet owes more to American West Coast libertarianism, communitarianism, European social democracy, or the ideas of contemporary business. What we can say is that the internet creates a space for convergence between broadcasters and newspapers, who now compete with each other directly on the World Wide Web. It is an open question where this leaves the state and its regulators vis à vis the underlying issue of the 'reliability' of the news. The technology seems to point in the direction of greater freedom, since the internet bursts wide open national jurisdictions of content regulation, but the evidence of contemporary debate and public opinion is that we may not be happy to see journalism left entirely to the market. We fear, in Onora O'Neill's words, that market forces alone may not prevent the poisoning of the wells of public discourse.

The effects of these waves of technological change upon the culture, ethics, and practice of journalism have already been profound. British law, for example, still today requires that all television and radio news services be politically impartial and accurate – and regulators have powers to intervene where this is not the case. Amid all the noise directed against the power in the UK media market of Rupert Murdoch, it is easy to overlook the extraordinary power of the BBC, a publicly owned body which controls half the radio market, almost 40 per cent of television, and has been among the largest, if not *the* largest, investor in on-line content in Europe. Some see these arrangements as a persistent mechanism for political or establishment control of the most powerful news medium, but it is perhaps more accurately seen as a deliberate, Gaullist denial of influence to the international market forces that continue to shape the press. Since research suggests that the British public trusts the news it gets from television more than it trusts what it reads in newspapers, politicians are justified in claiming that there is public support for these arrangements. In the United States, by contrast, the most serious alarm about the decline in journalistic quality relates to television, and especially to the decline in the news divisions of the television networks. Is it possible that Americans will lose faith in the deregulatory course followed by all administrations since President Reagan's? If not, how will American journalism develop a response to its critics? Will the market be judged capable of delivering satisfactory solutions?

What cannot be denied is that the new digital technologies have started to cause radical shifts in the ways in which everyone consumes news. That is true of the elderly Afro-Caribbean ladies I watched sitting in the public library in Peckham, South London, on a rainy Saturday afternoon reading the *Jamaica Gleaner* newspaper, on-line. It is also true of Arab communities around the world, which can today access via satellite and cable television systems a number of global Arabic-language television news services, such as Al Jazeera, which became well known after the terrorist attacks on New York and Washington in September 2001. These newcomers present a serious challenge not only to the hegemony of global news services owned by Americans or former colonial powers like Britain and France but also to the authoritarian regimes which hold sway in most Arab countries.

At the same time, many ethnic and linguistic diasporas are finding that they can defend their cultural identities, or even acquire muscular new ones, as a direct result of enhanced media connectivity. Take the example of Wales, a tiny country on the very edge of Europe with a population of 3 million people, of whom approximately one-fifth speak Welsh, one of Europe's oldest but least widely spoken languages. Today, as a result of investment by BBC Wales in an on-line news service, that community has for the first time in its history an accessible, written daily news service, in effect an electronic daily newspaper, in the Welsh language. This is, naturally, very welcome to Welsh speakers, but it is not something that could possibly have been delivered on a commercial basis through ink-on-paper technology.

Today there are instant news services from all sorts of communities of interest, from cancer sufferers to anti-capitalist campaigners, the latter styling their own 'anti-media' organizations 'independent media centres'. 'Anyone with a modem can report to the world,' says Matt Drudge, the Hollywood-based internet journalist and gossip-monger, whose work precipitated crisis at the Clinton White House.

New news, new democracy

According to some commentators, this burgeoning supply of new services tells us that journalism, far from dumbing down to a bland irrelevance, is diversifying to an unprecedented health and influence. John Hartley, a British academic who works in Australia, calls journalism 'the sense-making practice of modernity', the very foundation of democratic politics and the primary wiring of popular culture. Hartley and others like him view the so-called 'tabloidization' of journalism not as a diminution of its ambition, but as an extension of its reach, another unfolding layer in the story of journalism's role as the oxygen of democracy.

These proponents of what is sometimes called the 'the new news' say that the 'concerned journalists' of the Ivy League American newspaper industry are simply failing to get the point that they are in the process of being swept aside by an interactive and so less rule-based type of journalism, that works via email, text-messaging, multimedia story-telling, web-logging, consumer magazines, popular music, and a host of other media yet to be invented. Rap music, it has been said, is 'the CNN black people never had'. The 'old news,' say the new news radicals, is like the old politics, simply not of any interest to younger people, and the old-timers should get on a new road if they can't lend a hand.

There are certainly figures to support this depiction of a *nouvelle vague* in news. By 2000, more than one in three Americans, and half of Americans under the age of 30, were going on-line at least once a week to pick up news. British research in 2002 found that the internet was regarded as the main source of news by a significant group of young British Asians, who do not consider themselves well served by mainstream news media. This same research, however, also found that the type of news gathered on-line was more global than local, and more concerned with sport and entertainment than with politics.

In the US, regular viewing of network television news fell from 38 per cent to 30 per cent of the population in the two short years between 1998 and 2000, as it was squeezed not only by the internet but also by cable news services. Newspaper consumption is falling very sharply among young people. In a recent survey, only 30 per cent of Americans in their thirties said they had read a newspaper the previous day, down from a figure of 53 per cent a decade earlier. This does not mean, however, that young people are not reading. The same survey showed that Americans under the age of 50 read lots of magazines and are as likely to have read a book as a newspaper the previous day. 'Young people are reading everything but newspapers,' says Andrew Kohut, director of the Pew Research Centre for the People and the Press.

This book is an attempt to describe and analyse the forces at work upon contemporary journalism and to judge the concerns of the defenders of 'old news' values against the enthusiasms of the 'new news' generation. I operate from the assumption that journalism matters not just to journalists, but to everyone: good journalism provides the information and opinion upon which successful democratic societies depend. Corrupt that and you corrupt everything. But, equally, let journalism ossify, or be economically undermined, and politics and public life will also suffer.

The discussion that follows entails some historical background, about the emergence of the idea of a free press, the rise of newspapers, radio, television and new media, and the growth of public relations, which was intimately connected with the development of both journalism and democratic politics in the last century. But this is not a history book. It is the reflection of a journalist who happens, in the last thirty years, to have enjoyed a rather unusual career, working all over the world, and in all media.

I started as a local newspaper reporter in northern England and spent a decade reporting for the *Financial Times*, one of the world's few global newspapers. I then ran the BBC's vast news and current affairs operation during a period of its reinvigoration in the late 1980s before becoming in succession: deputy editor of the *Financial Times* and editor of the *Independent*, a position from which I was fired at the end of 1995 for refusing to cut further an already emaciated editorial budget. That took me to the editor's chair of the *New Statesman*, a great political weekly, founded by Fabian Socialists nearly a hundred years ago, before I took time out for reflection in Britain's oldest journalism school at Cardiff, where I continued to make radio and television documentaries and write for newspapers.

Dead black babies

These diverse experiences have given me the privilege of working alongside some of the world's best journalists, for some of the world's best news media organizations. But I have also worked for a boss accused of serious dishonesty and I have encountered the worst kind of news room bullies, the sort of people who regard inquiring foreign journalism as inexplicable concern for 'dead black babies'. More recently, I have taken on a communications role inside a major UK business, where I have seen from a different vantage point the way that journalism works. I am also a board member of Britain's new regulatory body for the communications and media sectors, Ofcom, where our job includes grappling in a practical way with many of the issues discussed in these pages.

One thing I have learnt as a journalist is that all journalism is defined, to some extent, by the institutions within which it is created, and that every type of institution brings strengths and weakness to the mission of journalism. BBC journalism is magnificent in its range, carefulness, and resources, but it does tend towards an establishment view of the world. That is probably inevitable, given its funding structure and governance. Journalism on the *New Statesman*, by contrast, where our annual editorial budget would not have covered the taxi bills of a tiny division of the BBC, was about finding new ideas and new angles, missed by the mainstream press, in pursuit of a politically committed view of the world. What is obvious to anyone who has worked in journalism is that we need many and competing cultures of ownership if our news media are to be truly diverse and, consequently, as a whole, trusted. Non-diverse journalism cannot, by definition, achieve trust across the whole range of a public which is itself so diverse in terms of economic circumstance, class, ethnicity, gender, region, and in many other ways. Nor can a journalism which lacks diversity and plurality adapt to ceaseless change. If journalism cannot be both trusted and adaptable, it will fail.

It will by now be obvious that I did not set out to write this book entirely convinced by the arguments of the 'old news' people, the 'concerned journalists' of the United States. Whilst I have been raised with and share their commitment to old-fashioned virtues like accuracy and truth-telling in journalism, I suspect that there is in their response to the 'new news' something of the *ancien régime*, alarmed at the cry of the mob in the street. Matt Drudge, the bloggers, 24-hour TV news channels, 'investigative comedy' and even celebrity journalists and creative public relations are all part of the wave of energy and innovation which journalism and public communications constantly needs to refresh themselves: they may be part of journalism's necessary diversity, and self-interrogation, rather than its enemy.

Where we are all agreed is that fresh, trenchant, bracing journalism is the oxygen not only of democracy but of cultural exchange. The contest between the state, its citizens, and journalism, and the remaking of the terms of the relationship between them, is a relentlessly moving diorama. As John Keane, one of our best writers on democracy, has said: 'freedom of communications is an ongoing project without an ultimate solution. It is a project which constantly generates new constellations and dilemmas and contradictions.'

But the underlying mission of journalism itself does not change. It is to provide the information and argument that enables societies to work through their disagreements, to establish agreed facts and to know their priorities. And it is a job done well only when accomplished with style and impact: when the words flow and the pictures are immaculately sequenced. Unlike poetry, which as W. H. Auden said, 'makes nothing happen' and 'survives in the valley of its making where executives would never want to tamper', journalism strides out into the world and demands a response. Executives and politicians will always want to tamper with the work of journalists.

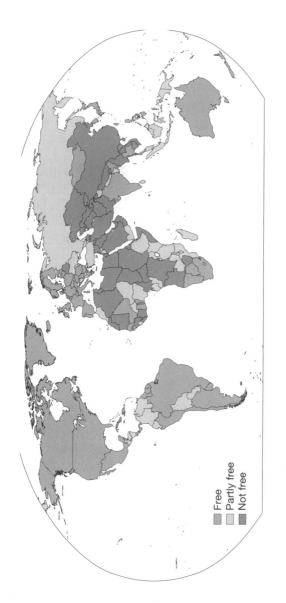

1. World Press Freedom Map. The modern struggle for press freedom is roughly 350 years old, but still campaigning organizations regard huge tracts of the world as lacking free news media.

Free
Partly free
Not free

Chapter 1

Born free: a brief history of news media

Journalism is not an easy business. In the year 2004 alone, 56 journalists were killed in the course of doing their jobs. It was the highest figure since 1994, when seventy-two journalists died. The running total for the decade stands at 337, not counting the large number of other media workers, such as researchers and translators, who also lost their lives.

Such deaths mostly go unnoticed. An exception was the case of Daniel Pearl, the *Wall Street Journal* reporter, who was murdered in such grim circumstances that it constituted a 'story'. Pearl, 38, had set out to understand the workings of militant Islamic networks in Europe following the suicide attacks on New York and Washington in September 2001. His inquiries took him to Pakistan, where he was kidnapped and held in captivity before having his throat slit on camera. The resulting videotape, showing a man brandishing a severed head, was then handed to American officials, to ensure that the murder made its maximum political impact. Pearl's pregnant wife said her husband had always felt impelled to go where the story led.

Of the other thirty-six journalists killed in the year of Pearl's murder, eight died in the space of a few weeks as American troops opened up the battle to take control of Afghanistan from the Taliban. There were more Western casualties among the media in this war than in the American-led alliance directing it. In the aftermath of the subsequent invasion of Iraq, kidnappings and on-video executions became a rebel stock in trade, several of them involving journalists. Deadlier still was the car bomb which exploded in October 2004 outside the Baghdad bureau of Al-Arabiya, a Saudi-owned television news channel based in Dubai. The explosion killed five employees and wounded 14 others, five of them journalists, and was followed by a claim from the 'Jihad Martyrs Brigades' that the attack should be seen as 'just a warning' about the station's reporting of the conflict. When democracy is at stake, journalism is in the firing line.

But it does not require a war for journalists to die. According to the Committee to Protect Journalists, most of the thirty-seven killed in 2001 'were murdered in reprisal for their reporting on sensitive topics, including official crime and corruption in countries such as Bangladesh, China, Thailand and Yugoslavia'. During the same, unexceptional year, the CPJ recorded 118 cases

DEADLIEST COUNTRIES

Country	Confirmed killings 1995–2004
Iraq	36
Algeria	33
Columbia	30
Russia	29
Philippines	22
India	16
Sierra Leone	15
Brazil	12
Afghanistan	10
Bangladesh	10
Mexico	9

2. Journalism is dangerous: this table shows the most dangerous countries for journalists in the last decade.

of journalists being jailed, mostly from 'little noticed crackdowns in Eritrea and Nepal, carried out after September 11,' which provided an excuse for despots all over the world to brand their political opponents as 'terrorists' unworthy of basic human rights. Nor are such outrageous events confined to faraway tyrannies. Veronica Guerin was shot in her car by gangsters in Dublin in June 1996. A year earlier, a masked man had entered her home, pointed a gun at her head and then shot her in the thigh. She carried on her investigations, with the comment: 'I am letting the public know exactly how this society operates.'

3. In the 'war against terrorism' journalists became targets, sometimes of 'friendly fire' and bombs, sometimes of hostage takers. Giuliana Sgrena, an Italian journalist, was seized in Iraq and eventually released. Others were not so fortunate.

According to those who map the state of world press freedom, that freedom is now measurably in retreat from the post cold war flood tide, when it still did not cover the majority of the world's land mass. In the new century, China has maintained its long reputation as the world's leading jailer of journalists and Russia, along with one or two other eastern European states, has slipped from a ranking of 'partly free' to 'not free'. Freedom House, the organization responsible for this survey work, identifies Burma, Cuba, Libya, Turkmenistan and North Korea as the world's blackest spots for free journalism. Optimists believe that, in due course, greater prosperity will foster democracy, education and greater media freedom. Pessimists ask whether there are deeper cultural forces in play against the West's post-Enlightenment assumption that identifies free journalism as the precursor of all political and economic liberties.

From Milton to the American Constitution

From an American and European perspective, history supports the case for optimism. Ask journalists from these continents (and others, such as Australasia where cultural roots are shared) their purpose and they will often give the standard reply: to hold power to account. Behind this momentous mission lie 350 years of passionately contested history. It is worth sketching the main contours.

The narrative starts with the Reformation, when Protestants split from the censorious authority of Rome, and runs through the English Civil War (1642–8), when republicans and dissenters toppled monarchists, spurred on by the first great tract in the cause of free expression, John Milton's *Areopagitica* with its radicalizing plea: 'Give me the liberty to know, to utter and to argue freely according to conscience, above all liberties.'

From there it was a small step to the first flowering of English journalism. Boosted by the abolition of pre-publication censorship, journalists such as Daniel Defoe, Joseph Addison, Richard Steele, Jonathan Swift, John Wilkes, and Thomas Paine became men of national and, in Paine's case, global influence. But it was not all revolutionary pamphleteering. We owe to Defoe a snapshot of the first professional reporters, working London's coffee houses in 1728 with a ruthlessly commercial craftsmanship. Defoe writes:

> 'Persons are employed ... to haunt coffee houses and thrust themselves into companies where they are not known; or plant themselves at convenient distances to overhear what is said ... The same persons hang and loiter about the publick offices like housebreakers, waiting for an interview with some little clerk or a conference with a door keeper in order to come at a little news, or an account of transactions; for which the fee is a shilling, or a pint of wine.'

Defoe's metaphor of the journalist as burglar sits tellingly with Janet Malcolm's contemporary depiction of the journalist as 'confidence man' referred to in the previous chapter. But whatever the ethical tensions latent in the emerging business of journalism, a free and vigorous press was an increasingly potent aspect of the political, economic and cultural landscape of the British Isles. When the London media industry located itself in Fleet Street, a dingy thoroughfare connecting the capital's business district to the east with the seat of political power in the west, it staked its claim to a unique power base.

Thomas Paine's contribution to our brief history surpasses even Defoe's. The son of a Norfolk stay-maker, Paine fomented revolution on both sides of the Atlantic. He sailed for Philadelphia in 1774 and two years later published *Common Sense*, a pamphlet setting out the case for American independence from British rule. A best-seller in America, it was also, according to a contemporary report, 'received in France and in all Europe with rapture'. The next year, Paine returned to England and wrote *Rights of Man*, arguing that human beings have a natural right to govern themselves, rather than to be governed by the beneficiaries of inherited title and power. Arraigned for treason, he fled to Paris and was elected a Deputy in the National Convention, before being swept aside by revolutionary factionalism, which led to his imprisonment and almost to his death. Paine then returned to the United States, where he lived out his days on the uneasy borderland between political power and journalism. He died in New York in 1809, refusing with his last breath to express any belief in the divinity of Jesus Christ.

Milton's spirit and Paine's didactic radicalism are written deep into the heart of the American Constitution and its First Amendment that: 'Congress shall make no law . . . abridging the freedom of speech or of the press', a momentously important linkage between the universal individual right of free expression and the liberties owing to the dominant news medium of the day. Thomas Jefferson reinforced the point when he wrote in 1787 to Colonel Edward Carrington the most comforting words in the history of journalism, that: 'The basis of our government being the opinion of the people, the very first object should be to keep that right; and were it left to me to decide whether we should have a government without newspapers, or newspapers without a government, I should not hesitate a moment to prefer the latter.'

Blood-stained newsprint

Amid the bloodier footprints of the French Revolution, Paine's influence is less easy to specify. This was a political maelstrom which thrust many journalists into often brief positions of public influence and, in some case, direct political office, with all the attendant risks. The editor of the *Ami du Peuple*, Jean Paul Marat, was murdered in his bath, leaving for posterity a copy of his newspaper stained with his own blood. One commentator has described the French

Revolution as 'journalism's big bang'; the point at which it started to become the pervasive engine of modern, democratic societies.

This mighty legacy touches French journalism today. France's journalism, with its roots in the political tract and the essay rather than the witnessed news report, tends to be more intellectually adventurous and serious than its Anglo-Saxon counterpart, but it is also less empirically forensic. French journalism is also more sensitive to the privacy of individuals: soft, say its Anglo-Saxon critics; grown up say its advocates. According to the historian Jack Richard Censer, the radical newspapermen of the French revolutionary period 'generally saw themselves as politicians with a primary responsibility to influence the course of events and with little allegiance toward any abstract journalistic ethic'.

An Asian model?

It is important to note, however, that the English and American newspapers which flourished in this long period of democratization were by no means the first in the world. China, for example, had official information sheets (*tipao*) centuries before the years of revolution in Europe and America, spawning unofficial rivals of sufficient journalistic enterprise that the Sung dynasty (960–1279) felt it necessary to suppress them. The attitude today of the Chinese authorities to news media freedom on both the Chinese mainland and in the former British colony of Hong Kong leaves a great deal to be desired from a western liberal standpoint, but the history and culture of these places can hardly be expected to lead to a replication of Euro-American news industry values. The history and cultural context of a newspaper like the *South China Morning Post*, which has flourished in its own way under British colonialism and re-accession by the People's Republic of China, indicates the complexities involved.

The resulting tensions are highly visible within a modern city state like Singapore, shaped by a post-colonial experience which has seen rapid and successful economic development, not least in the area of the new communications technologies. To Western eyes it is paradoxical that the Government of Singapore should simultaneously be committed to one of the most sophisticated communications infrastructures in the world, whilst also running a regime of censorship and media restriction, which has brought it into conflict with some of the west's most respected media companies, including *The Economist* and the *Wall Street Journal.*

The modern Japanese press, by contrast, enjoys the protection of a national constitution which enshrines the principle of press freedom, established under strong American influence after the Second World War, and is not subject to state censorship. But the workings of Japanese news media are barely recognizable to journalists from the United States or Britain. Japanese society works more through negotiation, collaboration and consensus than through strong ideological difference and competition. Japanese journalists are bound together in a network of a thousand 'press clubs', all linked to major institutional or industrial sources of power and therefore of news. These clubs are designed to ensure that both sides play by a set of unofficial rules. It is, in essence, a form of self-regulation, designed to avoid embarrassment and misunderstanding, but which in the opinion of its (mostly Western) critics neuters and homogenizes Japan's journalism through the management of news flows.

On liberty

It is upon the intellectual foundations of European liberalism, however, that the edifice of the free press stands. In early nineteenth-century Britain, the liberal intelligentsia was in no doubt about the need to contest the more *étatiste* view of journalism they saw across the English Channel, just as they also contested a more Gallic *dirigiste* view of economic policy. James Mill, the Scots utilitarian, argued in an influential essay in 1811 that the dangers of a timorous press, too friendly to established political power, greatly exceeded the political dangers of its opposite. Mill thought the relative political stability of England, Holland, Switzerland, and the United States, compared with the bloody turmoil in France, resulted not from an excessively free press in France, but from an excessively controlled one. Almost half a century later, Mill's son, the philosopher John Stuart Mill, delivered the most eloquent case for political and economic liberalism in the English language. In his 1859 essay *On Liberty* he writes:

> 'The peculiar evil of silencing an expression of opinion is that it is robbing the human race; posterity as well as the existing generation; those who dissent from the opinion, still more than those who hold it. If the opinion is right, they are deprived of the opportunity of exchanging error for truth: if wrong, they lose, what is almost as great a benefit, the clearer perception and livelier impression of truth, produced by its collision with error.'

Liberals (in the English, historical meaning of that word, rather than its looser contemporary American usage) were thus the friends of press freedom, philosophically, politically and commercially. They opposed special taxes or stamp duties on newspapers as vigorously as they supported greater freedom to trade. The upshot was a proliferation of titles in what is often seen as the golden era of the British press: politically radical but not yet, in the early stages of the industrial revolution, narrowly corporate. Henry Hetherington's *Poor Man's Guardian*, launched in 1831, in defiance of stamp duty, declared: 'It is the cause of the rabble we advocate, the poor, the suffering, the industrious, the productive classes. . . . We will teach this rabble their power – we will teach them that they are your master, instead of being your slaves.' Yet only two years after the launch of *Poor Man's Guardian*, Hetheringon was also promising readers of his

Twopenny Dispatch a diet of 'murders, rapes, suicides, burnings, maimings, theatricals, races, pugilism and . . . every sort of devilment that will make it sell'. Thus did the lion of radical political journalism lie down with the lamb of tabloid sexploitation.

Before long, bigger newspapers, free from taxation and fat with advertising, were trumpeting the glories of a 'new journalism'. In 1852, *The Times* defined as its purpose: 'to obtain the earliest and most correct intelligence of the events of the time and instantly, by disclosing them, to make them the common property of the nation'. By now, papers like *The Times* were enjoying the greater news coverage made possible by the emerging news agencies, such as the one launched by Julius Reuter in 1851.

Government by journalism

In these circumstances, journalism asserted itself, pre-figuring the era of media hyper-power in which we now live. The embodiment of what Victorian intellectuals called the 'New Journalism' was W. T. Stead, editor of the *Pall Mall Gazette*, who specialized in controversial exposures of sex rackets, as a result of which he found himself in jail. It was in Holloway Prison, in 1886, that Stead wrote a remarkable essay on the future of journalism, informing the world that journalism had now become 'superior to that of any other institution or profession known among men'. For Stead, the journalist was the key to comprehending public opinion, 'to be both eye and ear for the community'. He concluded: 'I have not yet lost faith in the possibility of some of our great newspaper proprietors who will content himself with a reasonable fortune, and devote the surplus of his gigantic profits to the development of his newspapers as an engine of social reform and as a means of government.' A means of government? Stead was not kidding. Through 'an exhaustive interrogation of public opinion', such a newspaper would acquire an authority which politicians would be unable to ignore.

'The journalist would speak with an authority far superior to that possessed by any other person; for he would have been the latest to interrogate the democracy. Parliament has attained its utmost development. There is need of a new representative method, not to supersede but to supplement that which exists – a system which will be more elastic, more simple, more direct and more closely in contact with the mind of the people. . . . When the time does arrive, and the man and the money are both forthcoming, government by journalism will no longer be a somewhat hyperbolic phrase, but a solid fact.'

This early techno-utopianism foreshadows today's alarms about 'government by the media' and declining affiliation to institutions of representative democracy. Stead's hubris was in tune with an era when newspapers were launched not with soberly descriptive titles such as *The Times*, *The Gazette*, and *The Record*, but ablaze with popular aspiration: the *Mirror*, the *Sun*, the *Comet*, and the *Star*. Most of Britain's great popular newspapers of today were born in the final years of Queen Victoria's reign: the *Daily Mail* (1896), the *Daily Express* (1900), and the *Daily Mirror* (1903). Parallel forces were at work in the United States, where proprietors like William Randolph Hearst and Joseph Pulitzer were creating the so-called 'yellow' press. The newspaper industries of Britain and the United States entered the twentieth century at the peak of their political and economic power.

Media monopoly, communism and fascism

This heyday of the market-based, industrialized free press was, however, remarkably short-lived. Within a couple of decades of the new century, the market-based model for the development of news media came under challenge, first from radio, then from television and, towards the end of the twentieth century, from the internet. These were media which would soon acquire a reach never achieved by newspapers and they were born not in tiny printers' shops subject to the laws of a market economy; rather, they were inventions naturally and speedily commandeered by governments, which took the view that the new communications technologies must be owned or licensed by the state. It is too easily forgotten that the media technologies of the twentieth century have their roots not in markets, but in monopoly or licensed oligopoly.

The implications for journalism would be far reaching, as democratic governments sought new ways, either through direct control of the emerging technologies or through the medium of 'independent' regulatory bodies, to satisfy themselves that the news media would operate within a broadly defined and accepted public interest. As the twentieth century gave way to the twenty-first, and the technologies of analogue radio and television surrendered to digital communications technologies, making it possible for broadcast-type services to be transmitted globally and instantly

4. Tiananmen Square. Television has been frequently attacked for 'dumbing down' the news media, but when big events unfold, there is nothing to compare with the memorable drama of television news. Here, a student demonstrator halts a column of tanks in Tiananmen Square, during the famous protests in 1989.

across a range of infrastructures, new challenges would emerge. Now that newspapers, radio and television could share delivery platforms, via broadband internet, would it still make sense, or even be possible, to regulate them differently? If not, would the trend be in the direction of greater market-based freedom associated with the free press? Or would the new communications networks, in all their complexity, be regulated for content and standards by some state or political authority?

5 George Orwell was probably the twentieth century's greatest journalist. Not only did he write brilliantly and didactically about the art of clear writing, he also, in his novels *Animal Farm* and *1984*, imagined a dystopia in which the corruption of information systems would lead to tyranny and systematic violence. Today Orwell's Big Brother has taken on a more playful meaning, in reality television.

Chapter 2

Big brother: journalism and the altered state

In the early years of this century, I spent some time in Russia, talking to journalists from the length and breadth of that vast country. They had come together for an annual media seminar to imbibe good practice from democratic societies. In most respects, such evangelism can only be unreservedly welcomed. No one can defend the deceitful propaganda of the 'information regimes' of the Soviet era, when the titles of leading newspapers such as *Pravda* ('Truth') were turned into grim self-parodies. Yet, as I sat through the seminar, I couldn't avoid a sense of irony at the moralizing rhetoric of the (inevitably) Western evangelists at a time when Western journalism was widely felt to be struggling with its own diminished civic purpose. In 2002, as stock markets collapsed amid wave after wave of corporate scandal, it was by no means obvious that advanced capitalism's model of lightly regulated big business was providing a convincing model for sustaining free news media.

But the rhetoric of free market evangelists remains potent. Rupert Murdoch, whose global business has been built beneath its halo, has compared satellite television, in which he is a leading player, to the Magna Carta and the abolition of pre-publication censorship by the English Parliament in 1694. In 1993, Murdoch went further, declaring that the new communications technologies 'have proved an unambiguous threat to totalitarian regimes everywhere'. This was the spirit which saw news entrepreneurs, among them Murdoch's great rival Ted Turner, founder of the news network CNN, embark for Moscow in the early 1990s, convinced that their proposed new channels would both liberate their viewers and enrich their owners.

Russian journalism at the edge

In the early years of the new millennium, the situation looked a good deal more complicated. Here at a Soviet-era conference centre on the edge of snow-bound Moscow, senior figures from the Russian Parliament, the Duma, the state television authorities, and the Moscow press squared up to a group of young, but by no means inexperienced journalists from across Russia. At issue was the kind of journalism developing in Russia, as it struggled between the dizzying polarities of anarcho-capitalism and fading memories of Soviet certainty.

Irina Lukyanova, a former newspaper journalist, was at that time presenter of the main political current affairs programme of SkaT, a television station in Samara, in the Volga. I asked her what influence she had over who appeared on her show – the kind of issue often hotly contested in the West between producers and presenters. 'I am allowed to choose,' she replied, 'except for those who pay for their places.' Those who pay? 'Yes, there are usually a couple of seats for those who pay, mainly politicians or business people.' How much do they pay? 'About a thousand US dollars. The price is set by the advertising department.' A further indignity, she explained, was the role demanded of journalists like her during election periods by the powerful regional politicians who, along with business tycoons, had taken control of much of Russia's political life in the post-Soviet period. Journalists are pressured to work for the election campaign teams where, inside a few weeks, they can earn as much as in the rest of the year. Around election time, Irina, who is popular with her audience, said she was required to act as 'interviewer' for what in effect were party-political broadcasts – a clear conflict of roles. She had dealt with this situation by developing a 'cold and mechanical' style of interviewing for these occasions, the stance of a 'microphone holder' rather than a journalist. I asked her to demonstrate, using a spoon as a microphone. It was an impressively coded statement against a practice she bitterly resented, but which she felt she could not change.

In the newspaper world, life can be even tougher. Alexander Yakhontov was editor of a weekly paper, *Novaya Gazeta*, in a small city a few hundred miles south of Moscow. He made a start in journalism in 1991, during the warm spring which followed the ending of the cold war. Like most papers, *Novaya Gazeta* had begun life as a tiny cog in the Communist Party machine – the voice of the local Young Communist League. In its communist heyday, it recorded a meaningless, but impressive-sounding circulation figure of 50,000. Reborn, post-glasnost, as a title owned by its staff with what Yakhontov styles a 'public watchdog' role in its community, largely learnt from American example, the paper was by the end of 2001 struggling to sell 4,000 copies a week and had been subject to repeated bouts of harassment from the local governor. Official tactics included efforts to evict the paper from its offices, court action, and, for a period, the establishment of a rival paper with an almost identical name. When I asked Alexander Yakhontov about his hopes for the future, he replied: 'The intelligentsia needs independent opinion. I hope we shall survive, despite all the hardships.'

During that same trip, I also visited the huge Ostankino broadcasting complex on the edge of Moscow to meet some of the people at the centre of the battle for control of the now partially privatized Russian television system. A few weeks earlier one group of journalists had walked out of the country's third largest network, NTV, in order to set up shop on the other side of the complex with the rival TV6, which was later forced off the air-waves. This contest demonstrated that the Kremlin was still fixing television industry politics at the highest level. Yet I was also struck by the contrast between what I saw in the NTV news production suite that evening and what I had observed fourteen years earlier, when I had visited Ostankino as the head of a BBC News delegation to Gostelradio, then the monopoly Soviet broadcaster, just before the fall of the Berlin Wall. Arriving then at about 11 a.m., I was asked whether I would like to observe the rehearsals for that evening's main television news bulletin, which was to be read by a thick-set man in a shiny suit. 'How can you rehearse a bulletin so long before it goes on air, since you can't yet know what the main news items will be?' I enquired. 'We already have our script. It has been cleared,' my host replied. In Soviet Russia, breaking news conformed to the working patterns of bureaucrats. As usual, it began with an account of a visit to Moscow by a sympathetic foreign dignitary.

Fourteen years later, NTV's evening news led with a reheated allegation of Kremlin involvement in the bombing of a Moscow apartment block, which triggered, or had been used to justify, escalation of the war in Chechnya. This war, between the Russian state and a separatist movement, presented a huge challenge to emerging media freedoms in Russia, exemplified when Russian troops handed over Andrei Babitsky, a Russian journalist working for the US government-funded Radio Liberty, to rebel troops. President Putin had described Babitsky's reporting as 'much more dangerous than firing a machine gun'. As I entered the NTV newsroom, the first computer screen I saw displayed the Drudge Report, the American muck-raking internet site. That same day, revelations about sexual misdemeanours by an executive involved in the TV6–NTV row would appear on a Russian website specializing in what Russians call 'compromat' – sleaze. This may not be a utopia of free expression, but it is a very long way from the old *Pravda*, with its global network of dull writers trained to eat well and service the party line. As President Putin continues to tighten his grip on television, he will not find the process as

6. Beslan: as Russia attempted to construct a fragile democracy in the post cold war world, the Kremlin kept a tight grip on television. Its justification was the need to take a strong line against terrorists, like those who massacred schoolchildren in Beslan.

straightforward as his Soviet forebears, but that will not stop him from trying.

American self-doubt

If Russian journalism is going through what Americans like to see as a version of its own struggle two centuries earlier on behalf of democratic values, what are we to make of the current self-lacerations of American journalism, which sounds at its most extreme like a crisis in the very soul of liberalism? The flavour of the debate is captured in the title of James Fallows' book *Breaking the News: How the Media Undermine American Democracy*. Fallows made his name with this tract and went on to edit the news weekly, *US News and World Report*. Another example is *Trivia Pursuit*, a 1998 book by Knowlton Nash, a well-known Canadian broadcaster. Its subtitle is: *How Showbiz Values are Corrupting the News*. Arthur E. Rowse, a journalist who has served on the *Washington Post* and the *Boston Globe*, entitled his confessional: *Drive-by Journalism: The Assault on Your Need to Know*. According to Rowse, the new wave in journalism has corrupted journalism with reckless mergers, 'exploited the First Amendment for profit', trivialized coverage of politics and public life and become over reliant on publicists rather than reporting skills.

The most striking charge of this wave of critics is that the First Amendment, designed to guarantee the individual's and the press's right to free expression, has been hijacked in pursuit of commercial interests by the likes of the Disney Corporation and AOL–Time Warner, who are in business to enhance shareholder value by providing services of entertainment. Why, it is asked, should journalism placed at the service of a global entertainment conglomerate qualify for the protection of a First Amendment whose spirit was designed to support newspapers' mission to hold power to account? This is the turn of events dubbed by concerned American journalists 'a fundamental and epic change with enormous implications for democratic society'.

Public journalism fights back

One envisaged remedy for this state of affairs is a return to 'public journalism', sometimes called 'civic journalism', which emphasizes the importance of journalists working more closely within their communities and where possible taking responsibility for more than their reporting. For example, a local newspaper might put itself at the service of a programme of environmental improvement, or a drive for higher standards in local schools, using not only the conventional tactics of revelatory reporting and setting out conflicting opinions, but also through more deliberately constructive interventions: the dissemination of public information material, running competitions, working with schools, and so on. Public journalism seeks to widen news agendas, beyond the familiar territory of crime, social disorder, scandal and entertainment. It makes a direct appeal back to the democratic well-spring of the free press: brought into being to serve the citizen's need. Civil society, in this argument, emerges as a democratic centre distinguishable from, say, elected Government or other more obvious institutions of democratic socities. Fallows dresses his argument with a call for higher personal standards among journalists, who are urged to follow politicians by making transparent their financial and other interests, to re-build trust with a public which increasingly regards them as 'buck rakers' rather than muck-rakers.

Many themes intertwine in this 'public journalism' debate: some concern issues of media ownership and journalistic ethics dealt with later in this book. But when we place side by side our snapshots of American and Russian journalism today, the biggest question to emerge is this: what *should* we see as the desirable relationship between journalism and a democratic state and its agencies? Clearly, the answers in practice will depend a great deal upon the depth and nature of the democracy in any given state, but are the principles still clear enough at a time of rapidly changing media technologies?

This is complex terrain, involving as it does consideration of the changing relationship between big business and political power in advanced democracies like the United States. Many Americans see their own media model as a beacon of liberal principle and this is supported, for example, by the way that the independent American judiciary has, on many occasions, defended the principle of free speech in the face of Government pressure. Yet it is also true that the de-regulation of American broadcasting since the presidency of Ronald Reagan is blamed by many American journalists for the decline in the status of news, leading to a withdrawal of what NBC's long-serving presenter, Tom Brokaw, has called 'conscience money'. The opening created by this de-regulation for a fifth television network, Fox, controlled by the pro-Republican, economic liberal Rupert Murdoch, involved a piece of political and industrial manoeuvring aimed at re-balancing media forces in a conservative direction. It was paralleled in the UK in the 1980s by the emergence, during Margaret Thatcher's premiership, of Murdoch's BSkyB to challenge the broadcasting supremacy of the BBC which, like the American television networks, is regarded by political conservatives as irredeemably left of centre in its political and cultural attitudes. Does this represent a triumph of liberalism or a triumph of political dirigisme? The case can be made on both sides.

Convergent media

Today, convergence between the technologies of newspapers, telecommunications, broadcasting, and computers is bringing these issues and tensions into ever sharper focus, obliging everyone to rethink the structure of these regulatory arrangements. Britain is among those to have decided that the best approach (like the American) is to have a single point of regulatory authority for all systems of electronic communication, whilst leaving newspapers largely free to regulate themselves, except when it comes to mergers and acquisitions.

Rupert Murdoch continues to deploy his 'neo-liberal' argument that the emergence of new media platforms obliges government to withdraw from regulation and leave television, radio, and on-line journalism to follow the path of newspapers, determined by commercial market forces. But this is a long way from the current reality in Europe, where most countries, including the UK, have laws that require television news to be politically impartial, a stricture which applies to any broadcaster seeking a licence to transmit within their territory. Politicians of all parties tend to support this status quo and there is still evidence of strong public support for this type of content regulation. However, it should also be noted that those people least inclined to support continued regulation and public funding of this 'public service broadcasting' model are those who enjoy the widest range of choice in their television services through cable and satellite delivery. As multi-channel television and radio become the norm, it is therefore by no means a foregone conclusion that the late-twentieth-century approach to regulation of news standards will be maintained.

Today, television viewers in the middle of England, Germany or Turkey can pick up not only their own domestic news channels, but also a range of American and other services originating beyond the national borders, where regulatory standards differ greatly. In Britain, these newcomers include a number of Asian television stations, serving Britain's large Indian, Pakistani, and Bangladeshi population, along with the Arabic-language stations, Al Jazeera and Al-Arabiya. Another relatively new option for British audiences is Murdoch's own Fox News, created for the American market with the deliberate aim of redressing what its owner sees as the liberal/left tendency in American network news. According to Murdoch: 'the time will come when there will be no further need for impartiality rules for any of the media.' This argument will gain even more force as broadband internet starts to allow broadcasting via the telecommunications network, further challenging established structures of broadcast power.

Against this neo-liberal position stands most of Europe's Social

Democratic and Christian Democratic traditions, buttressed by powerful institutions like the BBC, which each year receives almost £3bn a year of public money to enable it, among other things, to supply a form of high-quality journalism not only throughout the UK and its regions, but also to the world. Mikhail Gorbachev has spoken of the way he depended upon news from the BBC at crucial moments in his own political career and it was from the BBC that Northern Alliance troops in the deserts of Afghanistan got their information in the war against the Taliban in 2002.

No bonfire of regulations tonight

So the global reality in the first years of the twenty-first century was not, as Murdoch predicted, a bonfire of broadcast regulation. Rather, what we started to see was a cautious lightening of the regulatory burden, aimed at improving investment flows and innovation in electronic communications generally, combined with a continued insistence on the state's right to sanction public investment in non-market-driven broadcasting and, where possible, to regulate for impartiality of news.

In emerging democracies like Russia, it has not been difficult for politicians to continue to exercise very significant direct influence over television and radio and in the European Union, it is a matter of established law that member states have the right to subsidize their broadcasters on public interest grounds, in ways impermissible in most industries. In some countries, notably France, this position reflects a long-standing and passionately articulated resistance to the Americanization of national cultures. This Euro-nationalism was neatly illustrated during the crisis at the media giant Vivendi in 2002, when the company's boss, Jean Marie-Messier, dubbed by his critics Maître de l'Univers Moi-Même, was evicted following his attempts, in effect, to transplant the company's heart to New York. At the same time, German politicians were scratching around in search of a 'German solution' to the problems of the Kirch Media group.

It would be wrong, however, to suggest that Europe has been immune to the pessimism which has characterized America's internal debate about journalism. Across Europe, falling turnout at elections has been linked to the failings of the news media, which are accused somewhat self-contradictorily of both dumbing down and failing to appeal to young people. Audiences to mainstream television news bulletins and to current affairs programmes have fallen steadily in the last decade, along with readership of newspapers. Voting levels in European Union elections fell from two-thirds to under half in the last twenty years and across Europe, there is talk of the 'vanishing young reader' of newspapers. In the British general election of 2001, only 59.4 per cent of those entitled voted, the lowest figure since women got the vote. Among 18 to 25 year olds the figure was 39 per cent. Following this, the BBC quickly launched an internal inquiry about its own programmes, debating the premise that 'neither politicians nor media are truly in step with the mood of the nation'.

According to a wide range of critics and scholars, the problems of the European news media are very much of their own making. The French sociologist Pierre Bourdieu's study of television journalism found a system where 'all production is oriented toward preserving established values' and where competition 'rather than generating originality and diversity, tends to favour uniformity', though it is not clear from Bourdieu's argument whether the fault he finds lies chiefly with the market or the pervasive relationship between the French state and the country's electronic news media. What France has, says Serge Halimi, another left-wing critic, is 'media which is more and more ubiquitous, journalists who are more and more docile and a public information system which is more and more mediocre'.

The doyen of this leftist critique of journalism as an arm of established power is the American linguist Noam Chomsky, whose writings have had considerable influence upon writers like John Pilger, the Australian campaigning journalist. Pilger argues that

British television is just as parochial as American television and certainly does not spare the BBC from his characterization of a mass media functioning as a willing tool of a propagandizing political establishment. In Pilger's assessment, most journalists have become either puppets of tough proprietors like Rupert Murdoch or lazy and largely passive victims of public relations experts. They are pursuing a 'hidden agenda' – sometimes concealed even from journalists themselves. Nowhere is this more true, he would say, than in the reporting of war.

Chapter 3
The first casualty: journalists at war

'The first casualty when war comes is truth,' said Senator Hiram Johnson in 1917, an age of relative innocence in terms of the politics of mass media. War has indeed always delivered the most severe test of journalistic independence. Philip Knightley, who took Johnson's text as the title for his own history of war reporting, *The First Casualty*, argues that only in a 'war of national survival', such as the Second World War, should journalists entertain the idea of explicit cooperation with the state. Since most wars are not of this type, Knightley maintains that journalists cannot use this defence to justify weak or one-sided reporting. Given the constraints imposed by the military on war reporting, he concludes that it has become more or less impossible to do an honest job as a war reporter: 'The age of the war correspondent as hero is clearly over.'

Yet in situations where a newspaper or broadcaster knows that its own readers, or the children of its own readers, are risking their lives in a military action which falls short of a war of national survival, is it really possible for news organizations to behave even-handedly? In the 1991 Gulf War, for example, the news media prominently reported information about the likely allied counter-invasion of Kuwait, designed by military commanders to confuse the Iraqi enemy. If journalists had known this information to be wrong, would they still have been right to report it? Harder still, if a journalist had known the real, secret plan, would it have been correct to report that, even if it meant risking the loss of many of his own country's soldiers' lives? It is difficult to believe that any journalist rooted in a national community could answer yes to the second question.

Equally, however, you might think that even in a war of national survival, we would rather our journalists did not fall for crude propaganda, of the kind the British government used to such advantage during the First World War, circulating stories about German troops massacring babies and slicing the breasts from women as they advanced into Belgium. And when journalists on the ground can see with their own eyes that a military campaign is going horribly, chronically wrong, surely they have a wider responsibility to make this known, whatever the politicians may say about national interest. This is what happened when *The Times* revealed the disastrous state of the British army in the Crimean War in the 1850s and when American journalists exposed the atrocities and blundering ineffectiveness of their country's troops in Vietnam.

War in the living room

Yet it is obvious from a military perspective that media activity is there to be strictly managed, if not controlled. The Vietnam War was lost on television. When Britain went to war with Argentina in 1982 over the latter's incursions into the Falkland Islands, the only way journalists could get to the war or transmit stories from it was with the aid of the Royal Navy. As a result, there was hardly any front-line reporting until the very final stages of the conflict, when the outcome was no longer in doubt. Even so, the British government complained vigorously when London-based BBC journalists carried reports from Argentinian sources.

By the time of a series of conflicts in the 1990s in the Gulf and the Balkans, military planners had to deal with the fact that media

7. Saddam Hussain of Iraq invaded Kuwait in 1991, provoking war with the Western powers. The cable news company CNN made its name during the war, with its since much-imitated round the clock coverage.

technology had moved on. Now, television journalists could operate in the field with lightweight cameras which made it possible to shoot pictures and edit and transmit them from the field via satellite. The internet meant that when a radio station was bombed, or shut down (as was the case with the Belgrade station B92 in the Yugoslav wars), it could still reach listeners via the World Wide Web. By the late 1990s, news was happening around the clock on radio, television, and the internet. The days of a single, orderly news briefing a day, timed to serve the main evening news on television, was well and truly gone. In the Balkans, NATO quickly concluded that it would need to learn from the politicians of the Clinton and Blair era the techniques of spin, rapid rebuttal, and 'feeding the beast' – a technique designed to ensure that the 24-hour news media never suffer from the kind of hunger that encourages them to go looking for inconvenient stories and angles. 'Information' of dubious provenance about atrocities committed by the Serb armed forces on citizens of Kosovo were lent official support, only to be confirmed as false when the conflict ended and the 'information' about mass graves could be checked.

Embeds, or in-beds

The Kosovo War of 1999 also spread literally to the World Wide Web, when hackers from different factions tried to disrupt each other's web-based communications. The new openness of the communications system had other, startling effects. I recall sitting in a barber's shop in London during the early days of the allied bombardment of Belgrade and being taken aback to hear on a television phone-in the voices of people whose towns and cities aircraft financed from my taxes were bombing. Meanwhile, the BBC News website, at the time the most visited news site in Europe, included direct hyperlinks to sites devoted to distributing information and propaganda on behalf of the Serb authorities, without apparent complaint from the authorities. As General Wesley Clark, supreme commander of NATO's forces during the war, commented: in future all wars would be fought on the assumption that the news media operate behind enemy lines. The military response to these circumstances, as evident during the 2003 Iraq War, has been to promote the concept of 'embedding' reporters with troops, ensuring a level of military control but offering TV news organizations access to genuine, front-line pictures, often in real time. The war against Saddam Hussain prompted a major debate about the role of the 'embeds' (or 'in-beds' as their critics styled them) against the so-called 'independents' who were often far away from front-line military action, but arguably had more freedom to comment and make judgments. A post-war analysis of the experience conducted by the Cardiff University journalism school concluded that embeds provided 'a useful addition to the mix' of war reporting, but that their operation was associated with 'a greater disregard for the welfare of independent journalists, particularly by US forces.'

Even bombs can bore

Yet instant, continuous news has also yielded perverse effects. With news everywhere, the public attention span has shortened even in time of war. Faraway wars, which scarcely involved military casualties on the NATO side, could be mined for the most exciting bits, then forgotten as was the case when the dreary, routine bombing of northern Iraq continued year after year in the late 1990s and was barely reported in the Western media. The public was, no doubt, astonished to be told in 2002, as President George W. Bush talked up the idea of a decisive war against Iraq, that the First Gulf War had never, entirely, ended.

Editors were increasingly conscious that their readers, listeners, and viewers needed to be kept entertained and that hard news alone would no longer sell papers. This change was startlingly evident on the day when NATO bombers attacked Yugoslavia on 24 March 1999, the first NATO action on European soil since the end of the Second World War. The following day, only one British newspaper, the *Daily Telegraph*, thought the news justified clearing its front page for the event. The others all reported the news prominently, but felt they must offer other diversions for their readers. *The Times* obliged with a page 1 trail for a feature on the writer Bruce Chatwin's love affair with style-guru Jasper Conran. The *Guardian*'s preferred distraction was 'Doctors – the new fertility gods' and the *Independent*'s an item on England football managers. In the week prior to the bombing, the proportion of each paper's space given to foreign news ranged between 8 and 12 per cent for the white broadsheets and between 0 and 4 per cent for the tabloids. Of the British newspapers, only the *Financial Times*, serving a globally minded business reader, has stood outside the trend of dramatically diminished weight of foreign news in the editorial mix.

8. When NATO launched air and missile strikes against Yugoslavia in March 1999, it was the first allied action on European soil since the end of the Second World War. But British newspapers didn't regard the event as a 'clear the front page' story: they felt that, even in a war, readers would still want a range of softer items, in the case of the *Guardian*, newspaper of the year, items on fertility treatment and romantic intrigue.

The Bin Laden tapes

The war in Afghanistan in 2001/2 raised different issues, involving a self-styled 'war against terrorism'. Faced with this threat, the British and American governments made explicit demands on their news media not to broadcast videotaped messages from the presumed terrorist leader. In their coverage of the 'war against terror', news organizations vied with each other not only to be first with the news, but to declare their patriotism. Reporters wore patriotic badges in their lapels and NBC News's corporate symbol of the peacock acquired a stars and stripes embellishment. With the *New York Times* devoting space for many weeks to an acclaimed series of stories about the victims of Ground Zero, some wondered aloud whether it was possible for even this illustrious newspaper to maintain a detached and critical eye on the course of American foreign policy. There is no doubt that American journalism has

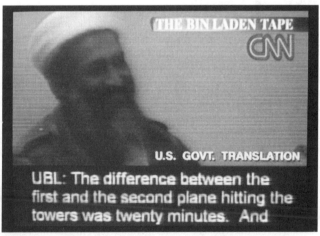

9. After the terrorist attacks on New York and Washington in September 2001, the Al Qaeda leader Osama Bin Laden supplied videotaped messages via the Arabic television station Al Jazeera. The British and American governments put pressure on broadcasters not to broadcast the tapes, but most did so.

grown progressively more parochial. In the last thirty years, the average soundbite on American television news has decreased from 42 seconds to 8 seconds and the proportion of time devoted to international news by US television networks has fallen from 45 to 13 per cent. American newspapers are not much better, having cut the proportion of their editorial space devoted to foreign news from around 20 per cent to 2 per cent in the last two decades. Chris Cramer, the former BBC journalist who at the time of 11 September was president of CNN International Networks, tried explaining what was going on to readers of *Le Monde*. 'In America, the competition for viewers has done little to enlighten the audience about the outside world, with most of CNN's competitors focussing on US news only: local crime and baseball scores, today's weather forecast, this week's lottery winners and the latest fad of so-called reality television.'

The rise of Al Jazeera

A significant outcome of the 'war on terror' was the emergence into public prominence of a number of Arabic language television services, of which the most striking was Al Jazeera. Established in the mid-1990s as an Arabic-language television service by the BBC, but eventually ditched when the BBC's Saudi partner pulled out, Al Jazeera is financed by the emir of Qatar from a base in Doha and is believed to be the most watched television channel among 300 million Arabs living in twenty-two countries around the world. Al Jazeera, and its direct rivals, present a rare challenge to the more or less complete global domination of English-language television news services, run by the likes of CNN, the BBC, Sky, and CNBC. It has, according to Nadim Shehadi of the Centre for Lebanese Studies in Oxford, also 'had an impact on the whole of the media in the region. The others are forced to catch up and compete – even the printed media. There's a lot more freedom now, because there's no point in controlling information if you know that people are going to find out from somewhere else.'

By 2002, Al Jazeera had a staff of 350 journalists, including fifty foreign correspondents in thirty-one countries, serving an estimated audience of 35 million. Its executives insist that it has imbibed its values of impartial reporting from the BBC, though its practice of describing Palestinian suicide bombers as 'martyrs' appears to many non-Arab observers to be an example of the violation of those standards. It was no surprise when the US Congress dug deep to fund a pro-American rival to Al Jazeera, Al Hurra, which has not been a popular success. More significant was the launch in 2003 of Al-Arabiya, part of a profitable group of Arab entertainment channels, based in Dubai and, crucially, supported by the conservative Saudis. 'Al Jazeera changed the way Arabs watch TV as much as the September 11 attacks changed Americans,' say the authors of a book on the news service. *The Economist* agrees: 'satellite television has created a sense of belonging to, and participation in, a kind of virtual Arab metropolis. It has begun to make real a dream that 50 years of politicians' speeches and gestures have failed to achieve: Arab unity.'

Lord Hutton concludes

It is impossible to conclude a discussion of war reporting without mentioning the events which, in 2003/2004, convulsed British politics and the BBC, ending with the resignation of the two most senior figures at the corporation, the Director General Greg Dyke and the Chairman Gavyn Davies.

In truth, the affair was only co-incidentally about the Iraq War, turning as it did upon a BBC radio report accusing the Prime Minister's office of deliberately 'sexing up' a dossier of evidence used to justify British participation in the American led invasion. The true context for the story was the decades-old running battle between the BBC's view of its own editorial independence and the frustration of successive Governments at hostile reporting.

In this case, the drama reached bursting point when the apparent

The Daily Telegraph

No 45,488   FINAL

www.telegraph.co.uk

Britain's biggest-selling quality daily

Wednesday, September 12, 2001   90p

War on America

Picture: SPENCER PLATT/GETTY IMAGES

Inside
Weather page 9
TV & Radio pages 22,23
Business pages 24-27
Sport pages 29-32

The Daily Telegraph 12-4-01

THE United States was on a war footing last night after the most devastating terrorist attack in history.

Two hijacked passenger airliners crashed into the twin towers of New York's World Trade Centre. Both towers collapsed with the loss of thousands of lives, sending out great clouds of thick dust that covered buildings and people in the streets like volcanic ash. Lower Manhattan was evacuated and the New York skyline changed for ever.

Minutes later in Washington DC a third hijacked aircraft crashed into the Pentagon, the heart of America's military machine. A fourth, believed to be heading for the presidential retreat Camp David, crashed near Pittsburgh.

The atrocity was meticulous in its co-ordination and horrifying in its effect.

A global television audience watched in disbelief as live footage showed the second plane hitting the Trade Centre minutes after the first.

Land borders were closed and airspace cleared of all but military aircraft as US forces were put on "high alert".

Financial centres were paralysed when Wall Street closed and shares plunged across world markets. The departments of Justice, State, Treasury, Defence and the CIA were all evacuated.

President Bush was flown to a bunker in Nebraska before returning to the White House. He pledged: "Make no mistake, we will hunt down and punish those responsible for these cowardly acts."

Reports: Pages 2, 3, 4, 5, 6, 7, 8, 9 and eight-page supplement. Comment: Pages 18 & 19

10a.

14. 42 Uhr (MESZ) beginnt das Grauen. Die Welt hält seitdem den Atem an

● Terroranschläge auf Manhattan, das Pentagon, das US-State Department ● World Trade Center dem Erdboden gleichgemacht ● New York weiträumig evakuiert ● Präsident Bush wurde mit einer Regierungsmaschine an einen geheimen Ort gebracht ● Die Welt ist geschockt ● Identität der Attentäter noch unklar ● Freudentänze in Palästinensergebieten ● USA kündigen massive Vergeltung an ● Lufthansa streicht alle Flüge nach Amerika ● Russland ordnet Gefechtsstufe 1 an ● Kanzler Schröder ruft Bundessicherheitsrat ein ● Nächtliche Krisensitzung des NATO-Rates in Brüssel: 21.20 Uhr – für alle Einheiten des Bündnisses wird höchste Alarmstufe angeordnet

Krieg gegen Amerika

Zehntausende Tote

Das Ende des World Trade Centers in New York

Die weltberühmte Skyline von New York gestern Nachmittag

10b. When terrorists crashed heavily laden aircraft into the
World Trade Center towers in New York on September 11 2001,
headline-writers around the world quickly converged on a theme:
War on America.

source of the BBC story, a Ministry of Defence official, slit his wrists on a country walk, so precipitating a full scale judicial inquiry into the offending news item. The presiding officer at the inquiry, Lord Hutton, concluded that the report had been mistaken on a number of points and severely criticized the BBC for the way it responded to the Government's complaints. Although some newspapers dismissed the Hutton report as a 'whitewash' and public opinion quickly moved behind the BBC, following the resignations, there is no doubt that the report and its subsequent investigation involved a series of errors.

The Hutton report, in truth, stands as no more than a footnote in the history of war reporting. Its place belongs more to the argument between journalists and politicians about the breakdown in trust between themselves and the public – a 'three-way' breakdown, as it has been called. These themes of political communication, 'spin-doctoring' and the journalistic response are discussed further in the chapters which follow. Lord Hutton's biggest contribution to the debate on these matters was his forensic description of the way the BBC and government communications work: a rare glimpse of the machine of journalism with its back off.

Chapter 4

Star-struck: journalism as entertainment

Journalism has always entertained as well as informed. Had it not done so, it would not have reached a mass audience. But today, say journalism's critics, the instinct to amuse is driving out the will, and depleting the resource, for serious reporting and analysis. Obsessed with a world of celebrity and trivia, the news media are rotting our brains and undermining our civic life.

There is no shortage of evidence. For Earth Day 2000, ABC News invited the dashing young actor and environmental campaigner, Leonardo DiCaprio, to conduct an interview with President Clinton for a prime-time network news show: a violation of journalistic values both on the grounds of DiCaprio's unfamiliarity with the art of rigorous interviewing and his partisanship on the subject, but justified by the network on the grounds of engaging a younger audience. A related technique was used during the 1997 British general election when leading politicians, including the future Prime Minister Tony Blair, were interviewed for BBC television by stand-up comedians and other entertainers. Gordon Brown, Britain's stern Chancellor of the Exchequer, was subsequently interviewed about British membership of the euro by a game-show hostess. Meanwhile, across the world, newspapers have piled into the infotainment mêlée, competing to secure columns written in the name of the latest TV celebrity chef, gardener, or interior decorator. It is said that the highest paid writer in British newspapers is not a journalist at all, but the astrologist Jonathan Cainer, whose popular predictions have been placed at the service of circulation drives by a succession of titles in recent years. Celebrities, quite simply, attract audiences.

At its most successful, the celebrity system is even capable of inventing its own stars through specially concocted media events. 'Reality television' shows, like *Survivor*, *Big Brother*, and *Pop Idol*, generate stars, who can be interviewed on breakfast news shows and featured, day after day, via magazines, newspapers, mobile phone systems and websites. Often this alternative 'reality' appears to outpunch reality itself in today's mass media, sometimes comfortingly so. As the American satirical magazine and website, *The Onion*, put it in a headline just a month after the 11 September attacks on Manhattan and Washington: 'Shattered Nation Longs to Care About Stupid Bullshit Again.'

To critics like Neil Postman, this is a prophecy triumphantly vindicated. Postman's 1985 book *Amusing Ourselves to Death* made the case that television is, by its nature, a medium of entertainment, and that as it displaces print as the primary medium of news, it is bound to result in a less-informed and less alert public. 'Dumbing down' is the phrase frequently used to label this phenomenon. Television news, Postman says, with its music, drama, and glamorous personalities, 'is a format for entertainment, not for education, reflection or catharsis'.

Yet this is no open-and-shut case. Television news is, especially in countries where it has been protected by strong regulation and benefited from massive public investment, regarded by most people not only as their main source of news but also their most trusted source. Those who watch, say, BBC television news get coverage of international events which far surpasses anything available in a mass-selling newspaper. Might it be that today's proponents of 'tabloid tv' are merely following the path their tabloid newspaper forebears did in the middle of the last century: namely widening access to news and topical debate?

The tabloid instinct

The tension between the serious news instinct and the entertainment instinct certainly isn't new to journalism. When William Randolph Hearst launched his *New York Mirror* in 1924 to take on America's first successful daily tabloid, the *New York Daily News*, he declared that the *Mirror* would provide '90 per cent entertainment, 10 per cent information – and the information without boring you'. If we are to understand so-called 'tabloid television', we need to consider the history of tabloid newspapers, which emerged to meet the demand of the literate urban working class in the late nineteenth century and which have constantly challenged our definition of journalism and its standards.

Strictly speaking, a tabloid is a newspaper page exactly half the size of a broadsheet page: a mathematical relationship which stems from the fact that publishers need to be able to print tabloid and broadsheet newspapers on the same printing presses. It is, in all sorts of ways, a misleading handle since the British tabloids which have given the term its contemporary meaning, the *Sun*, the *Daily Mail*, the *Daily Express*, and the *News of the World*, all began life as broadsheets and turned tabloid, respectively, in 1969, 1971, 1977, and 1984. The situation was complicated in 2003, when the up-market *Independent* and *Times* also went tabloid, even though they demurely preferred to use the word 'compact.' It is also important to note that in many countries, the most respectable newspapers have long been tabloids, *Le Monde* and *El Pais* among them.

Modern tabloid journalism, although it has spread across Europe in titles like Germany's *Bild-Zeitung*, is largely a product of transatlantic cross-pollination between Britain and the United States. It is worth sketching this history because it reveals the extent to which this tradition in newspapers has always blurred the line between fact and fiction, information and entertainment.

One of the earliest tabloid manifestos, written by T. P. O'Connor for the launch of an evening paper, *The Star*, proclaimed a journalism 'sometimes humorous, sometimes pathetic; anecdotal, statistical, the craze for fashions and the arts of housekeeping and, now and then, a short, dramatic and picturesque tale'. But mass-selling journalism could also be political, as Northcliffe's *Daily Mail* demonstrated in its attacks on the British commander-in-chief Lord Kitchener during World War One or in Beaverbrook's maverick politicking through the *Daily Express*, which earned a famous rebuke from Prime Minister Stanley Baldwin that newspaper publishers possess 'power without responsibility – the prerogative of the harlot throughout the ages'. Beaverbrook's erratic political judgement was illustrated when on 1 October 1938, the *Express*'s front page declared: YOU MAY SLEEP QUIETLY – IT IS PEACE FOR OUR TIME. Two days later, Hitler invaded Czechoslovakia.

Silvester Bolam, the *Mirror*'s editor from 1948 to 1953, felt no need to apologize for a louder, brasher style of journalism, announcing on his first front page: 'The *Mirror* is a sensational newspaper. We make no apology for that. We believe in the sensational presentation of news and views . . . as a necessary and valuable service in these days of mass readership and democratic responsibility.' Sensationalism, Bolam said on a later occasion, 'means the vivid and dramatic presentation of events so as to give them a forceful impact on the mind of the reader. It means big headlines, vigorous writing, simplification into familiar, everyday language, and wide use of illustration by cartoons and photographs.' By 1967, under the leadership of Hugh Cudlipp, the *Mirror* was selling 5.3 million copies a day, in a country with a population of 50 million.

Murdoch goes further

But by the late 1960s, the Mirror had a competitor snapping at its heels. The *Sun* first appeared in 1964, as a re-branded version of the trade unions' *Daily Herald*, but it was in deep trouble by 1969 when it was bought by Rupert Murdoch, the young Australian newspaper owner who had already purchased the *News of the World*, the naughtiest and best-selling of Britain's Sunday newspapers. Murdoch told staff that he wanted the *Sun* to focus upon 'sex, sport and contests.' One of its trade marks would be the 'page three girl' – a daily photograph of a naked woman. By the time the *Sun* soared past the *Mirror* in 1977, Murdoch was buying newspapers in the United States, first in Texas, then, in 1976, the *New York Post*. In Britain, faced with a challenge from the *Daily Star*, Murdoch brought in a new editor, Kelvin Mackenzie, who combined an ability to stretch the limits of taste and journalistic ethics with a passionate advocacy for the newly elected Margaret Thatcher, whose backing Murdoch would need as he developed his television ambitions in the UK.

By the time of Margaret Thatcher's war against Argentina in 1982, Murdoch and Mackenzie were well into their stride. The *Sun's* famous headline GOTCHA over the story of an Argentinian warship torpedoed by a British submarine resonated, even though it was never entirely clear whether Thatcherism had got Murdochism, or vice-versa. Mackenzie's *Sun* was often brilliant and equally often boorish. During the Falklands War, the *Sun* published an 'interview' with the widow of a dead serviceman with whom the paper had never spoken. Seven years later, the paper apologized for a front-page story headlined THE TRUTH, which accused Liverpool football fans of urinating on rescue workers as they tried to save people in a stadium disaster in which ninety-six fans were crushed to death.

Sometimes, Mackenzie's front pages arose from a world of pure make-believe. There is no other explanation for headlines like the

11. Freddie Starr ate my Hamster. Oh no he didn't. Tabloid newspapers frequently invent stories for the entertainment of their readers, or run with what might charitably be described as fanciful headlines. This classic in the *Sun* related vaguely to a stunt two years previously in which Starr, a comedian, pretended to eat a hamster.

famous FREDDIE STARR ATE MY HAMSTER, in March 1986, referring to an obscure incident two years earlier, when a comedian pretended to eat a hamster in a sandwich as a joke. On many days, it was impossible to tell the difference between the *Sun*'s reports of death or adultery in a popular television soap opera and similar dramas in real life. In the 1990s, the *Sun*'s star columnist, Richard Littlejohn, habitually concluded his ranting columns with the exasperated catchphrase: 'you couldn't make it up.' But at the *Sun* you could and they did.

Mackenzie's *Sun*, however, did not invent tabloid make-believe. The standard bearer in that regard was the *New York Enquirer*, which changed the course of tabloid history when it was bought in 1952 with a circulation of 17,000, by Generoso Pope Jr.

The tabloid Pope

Pope, who knew and admired the *News of the World*, renamed the paper the *National Enquirer*, turned it tabloid and told his small team of journalists to concentrate upon lurid crime stories. Fifteen years later, having acquired a slew of competitors, the *Enquirer* was selling a million copies a week. By 1975, pioneering the technique of selling at supermarket check-outs, circulation hit five million. In 1978, an edition of the *Enquirer* featuring a photograph of the corpse of Elvis Presley sold seven million copies, a peak not since exceeded.

Like all good tabloids, Pope's journalism had moments of high political impact. It was the *Enquirer*'s photograph in 1988 of presidential candidate Gary Hart on board a yacht called *Monkey Business*, with a young woman called Donna Rice, that ended Hart's political career. But countless other stories were simply made up. The culture of the most extreme tabloid 'newspapers', such as *News Extra* and *Midnight*, was closer to satirical comics like *National Lampoon* or *The Onion*, which are manifest self-parodies of journalism, than to mainstream newspapers. How many of the *Enquirer*'s readers actually believed a headline like HITLER SEEN ALIVE IN US or JFK ALIVE ON SKORPIOS (complete with picture) is a matter of conjecture. But no doubt the odd reader was taken in for a moment by one or other of the following freak-show offerings: SEVEN-HOUR ENEMA TURNS BLACK GIRL WHITE!, or MOM CLEANS KIDS BY PUTTING THEM IN CLOTHES WASHER? Or, GIRL, 16, BECOMES A GRANDMOTHER? The closer tabloid invention interplays with news of the real world, the greater its frisson.

Bill Sloan, who worked on the *National Enquirer* and other tabloids, has explained how experienced writers and editors like himself 'were routinely able to shift gears between out-and-out trash and serious reportage. One day they were inventing bogus stories for *News Extra* or even grinding out soft-core porn for the *National Bulletin*. . . . The next day, they were interviewing real people, writing legitimate articles, and striving mightily for documentation and credibility.' Sloan's justification for this, apart from the excellent salaries which attracted journalists to 'Tabloid Valley' in Florida, was that they 'had rediscovered a basic truth about their profession. They recognized early on what William Randolph Hearst had figured out eighty years earlier and what practically every TV news executive and major-daily editor realizes today – what qualifies as hot news has only the sketchiest relationship to pure information. For all their lofty pretences, today's mainstream media are essentially just another branch of show biz.'

Faking it

Sloan's explanation, logical enough, for the decline of tabloid circulations in the 1980s and 1990s is that all newspapers, along with most television, had by then muscled into the tabloid game. One illustration of this trend has seen British broadsheet newspapers publishing fictional columns, mostly with comic or satirical purpose, but occasionally misjudging the ability of their readers to get the joke. In one column, the writer, a well-known television satirist, pledged to commit suicide. The same writer, Chris Morris, used his television show to lure celebrities into invented schemes and situations designed to inflict public embarrassment on them. Apologists for this genre of television sometimes call it 'investigative comedy'.

"All the News
That's Fit to Print"

The New York Times

Copyright © 2003 The New York Times

VOL. CLII . . No. 52,506

NEW YORK, FRIDAY, JUNE 6, 2003

ONE DOLLAR

Times's 2 Top Editors Resign After Furor on Writer's Fraud

By JACQUES STEINBERG

Howell Raines and Gerald M. Boyd, the top-ranking editors of The New York Times, resigned yesterday morning, five weeks after the resignation of a reporter set off a chain of events that exposed deep fissures in the management and morale of the newsroom.

In a hastily arranged gathering in the newsroom on its third floor, the newspaper's publisher, Arthur Sulzberger Jr., told staff members that he wanted to "apologize to Howell and Gerald for putting the interests of this newspaper, a newspaper we all love, above their own."

Mr. Sulzberger said that Mr. Raines, 60, who was the paper's executive editor for less than two years, would be succeeded on an interim basis by Joseph Lelyveld, 66, his immediate predecessor, who retired in 2001. There will be no immediate successor for Mr. Boyd, 52, who was the paper's managing editor.

A spokeswoman for The Times, Catherine J. Mathis, said that the search for a permanent executive editor was likely "to move quickly" — other company officials said it could be a matter of weeks — and that candidates would be considered from inside and outside the paper.

For the staff members of The Times, the resignations yesterday set off a wave of emotions from sadness to relief, and prompted several dozen journalists to erupt in applause when informed of the departures of Mr. Raines and Mr. Boyd. The tumult had begun May 14 — three days after The Times had described in an extensive article how Jayson Blair, a staff reporter, had made errors or fabricated the equivalent of journalistic fraud in at least 36 articles since last October. Mr. Sulzberger told the newsroom staff

that he would not accept Mr. Raines's resignation if it were offered.

But in the days and weeks that followed, some of the newspaper's dissatisfaction with Mr. Raines was as deep as its most likely irreparable. Tensions were further inflamed when the paper became embroiled in a second controversy over the use of freelance reporters by Rick Bragg, a national correspondent close to Mr. Raines.

By Wednesday night, Mr. Sulzberger said in an interview, he and two editors had "a meeting of the minds, if you will."

"This was a decision that Howell and Gerald made, that I readily accepted," he said. "It was not precipitated by any specific event. It happened over a period of time."

"The morale of the newsroom is critical," Mr. Sulzberger said earlier yesterday. "The ability of reporters and editors to perform depends on their feeling they are being treated in a collaborative and collegial fashion."

The announcement of the two resignations came at midmorning, as many people were still arriving for work. Mr. Raines, standing on a microphone before dozens of reporters, editors, photographers and other newsroom staff members, many of whom sobbed audibly, said, "As I'm running late for my plane this time, I want to thank you for the privilege of being a member of the best journalistic newspaper in the world."

"It's been a tumultuous month, it seems," he added, "but we have produced some memorable newspapers."

He concluded by saying, "Remember, when a great story breaks out, go kick butt."

The remark, which could have

Continued on Page B8

12. Broadsheet journalists like to think that they operate to higher standards than their 'tabloid' rivals. But in recent years, a number of fakers have been exposed on the most highly reputed newspapers. One such scandal, in 2003, cost two senior editors on the *New York Times* their jobs.

Things do not look so funny, however, when high-profile conventional journalism also turns out to be infected with this easy-going relationship with facts. In 1996, a British documentary team working for Carlton Television faked sequences in a story about drug-running in South America, for which the company was fined £2m by the television industry regulator. Shortly afterwards, it emerged that the BBC was using actors to pose as people with problems on a daily talk show hosted by Vanessa Feltz. For journalists, producers and viewers, a world in which television documentaries move between conventional reportage, 'reconstructions' using actors, and 'docusoap' inevitably cause confusion, not least because television and film both have long traditions of drama 'based upon true life'.

In these ways, tabloid newspapers and television have played a big part in undermining trust between journalism and its audience. And the ethical rot involved has spread to the most high-minded newspapers in the world. In 1981, a young *Washington Post* reporter Janet Cooke was stripped of her Pulitzer Prize when it turned out that her award-winning story of child drug addiction was a work of imagination. Another newspaper columnist pretended to be suffering from cancer in order to make her column more engaging. More recently, Jayson Blair, a young black reporter on the *New York Times*, was exposed in 2003 as a serial faker of news stories, leading to his own resignation and that of two of the paper's most senior editors. Blair's later account of the scandal was tellingly entitled: *'Burning down my master's house'*.

Celebrities squared

In the same period that journalism has learnt to make light of the boundary between fact and fiction, it has also become increasingly absorbed by the entertainment and sales potential of celebrity, with significant consequences for the way that journalism is practised.

One especially damaging consequence is that, in order to get pictures and stories about celebrities, journalists have to deal with an industry of agents and publicists surrounding them, who make their own living from promoting the celebrity's brand values through obtaining the 'right' media coverage. This is a strictly two-way commercial play, because the news media know that the right celebrity on a magazine cover, or star interview on a talk show, can boost audiences and draw in advertisers. Celebrity is big money for everyone involved. It is inevitable that, in these circumstances, stories and pictures will be obtained not, chiefly, by the enterprise of reporters, but by those willing to pay the largest fees and guarantee the most favourable treatment for the star in question.

Generoso Pope discovered the power of celebrity when, in 1969, the *National Enquirer* published a family photograph of the late President Kennedy, surrounded by a story headlined: JACKIE BLASTED BY NURSE WHO BROUGHT UP JFK'S CHILDREN. Sales of the *Enquirer* increased by almost a third, prompting Pope to dispatch the following instruction to his staff: 'I want her on the cover at least every couple of weeks.' This they did, often embellishing pictures with stories of the purest fiction, claiming Mrs Onassis had changed religion, allowed her children to grow marijuana at home, and turned her second husband's hair white.

Much the same phenomenon attended the tragic figure of Diana, Princess of Wales, who entered global media consciousness in September 1980 when she was identified as the likely bride of Prince Charles, heir to the British throne. During the fairy-tale phase of the royal romance, the princess appeared on page one of the *Sun* sixteen times in a single month. When she chose to go on the BBC Television current affairs programme *Panorama*, in 1995, to discuss the breakdown of her marriage, the programme had the biggest audience in its history. No wonder the press was willing to pay huge sums for any snatched or even doctored picture of Diana, and that so many were on her tail as she sped into a Parisian underpass in August 1997.

SUNDAY Mirror

August 31, 1997 60p

SPECIAL EDITION

DIANA DEAD

Dodi killed too in Paris pile-up

DEAD: Diana

By Millicent Brown

PRINCESS Diana and her lover Dodi Fayed were killed early today in an horrific car crash in Paris.

Shocked eyewitnesses told how the inside of their limo was "full of blood" after the smash in a road tunnel, and how Dodi had been unsuccessfully given heart massage.

First reports said the couple's car could have been speeding to get away from pursuing paparazzi photographers who were trying to get pictures of them. The tragic couple had

Turn to Page 2

13. After her marriage to the Prince of Wales, heir to the British throne, Princess Diana quickly became one of the few celebrity faces guaranteed to push up newspaper and magazine circulations in markets all around the world. When she died in a Parisian road tunnel, pursued by press photographers, in August 1997, tabloid newspapers came under attack. At her funeral, the Princess's brother accused publishers of having 'blood on their hands'.

At her funeral, the princess's brother famously accused the press of having his sister's 'blood on their hands', whilst on the other side of the Atlantic, the *National Enquirer* was pulping its latest edition headlined: DI GOES SEX MAD: 'I CAN'T GET ENOUGH!' Disgusted by press behaviour towards the princess, other celebrities, including Madonna, George Clooney, Elizabeth Taylor, Tom Cruise, and Sylvester Stallone, called for stronger counter-attacks in the courts on the tabloids. But the trouble with the Diana affair, like so many other celebrity outrages, was that it was an act of collaboration with the enemy. In the late 1980s the *Sunday Times* was accused of printing lies about the troubled Charles and Diana relationship, based upon its expensive purchase of serialization rights to a book by Andrew Morton. It later turned out that Diana herself was Morton's primary source.

For the individual journalist, the celebrity boom raises another difficulty, in that celebrities, like any other individual in heavy demand, tend to be able to dictate the terms on which they do business. The result is that, when journalists are granted interviews with celebrities, they frequently agree to notify questions in advance and even to submit their copy for vetting prior to publication. Interviewees can also demand inclusion of references to commercial sponsors. This is a situation which makes the manipulations of the Westminster political lobby or the White House press corps look positively low-key. As Caroline Monnot of *Le Monde* protested during the French presidential election campaign in 2002, even the ultra-left candidate of Lutte Ouvrière was seen 'borrowing the tactics from movie stars' agents. Accreditations have to be applied for, there are waiting lists and you only get three timed questions with the star.'

Journalists as celebs

It is not surprising that some journalists who mix frequently with celebrities become pampered and wealthy celebrities themselves. Barbara Walters of ABC became the first million dollar news

presenter in the mid-1970s. Since then, the salaries of news presenters have multiplied tenfold and, like sports stars, actors and models, some appear to be heavily concerned with maximizing the value of their brand, whether on the lecture circuit, opening supermarkets, hosting executive conferences, or even associating themselves with product sponsorship. News executives defend these arrangements by saying that the public is attracted by celebrity: this is what it takes to get people to pay attention to news.

There is truth in this argument, but it is also true that the rise of celebrity journalism has been accompanied by sharp cuts in other, more expensive activities, such as newsgathering, especially overseas. Why would an American TV news service keep a well-informed but unglamorous foreign reporter in London, New York, Rome, or Tokyo if, when there's a big story, the audience 'wants to see' the star anchor live from the news scene? But anyone who knows anything about journalism will tell you that fly-in, fly-away stars are no substitute for reporters who know the terrain and who can make judgements based upon extensive off-air inquiry. In these days of instant TV news, it is not unusual for an on-the-spot reporter to be given the latest news he is supposed to be 'reporting' via email from head office, enabling the 'reporter' to stand in front of the camera and pretend that he or she has just discovered this information on the spot. Another, inevitable vice of celebrity television journalism is that it favours looks rather than journalistic acumen. Set this alongside the *Washington Post*'s desk-book or guidelines on 'the reporter's role,' which reads plaintively: 'Although it has become increasingly difficult for this newspaper and for the press generally to do so since Watergate, reporters should make every effort to remain in the audience, to be the stagehand rather than the star, to report the news, not to make the news.' Or note these comments by Richard Sambrook, a former Director of BBC News: 'On-screen talent, not content, is becoming the basis of difference between rival American news broadcasters and we are starting to see those same pressures in Britain.' Or, as Don Hewitt, creator of the CBS current affairs show *60 Minutes*,

has remarked: 'We want the companies we work for to put back the wall the pioneers erected to separate news from entertainment, but we are not above climbing over the rubble each week to take an entertainment-size pay cheque for broadcasting news.'

The tabloid decade

The case for tabloid journalism is that it can widen access to politics and other serious subjects. In the words of the young Rupert Murdoch: 'The *Sun* stands for opportunities for working people and for change in this society. It's a real catalyst for change, it's a very radical paper.' The same point can be made with respect to a famous incident in the history of 'tabloid television', the coverage in the mid-1990s of the trial of O. J. Simpson, the black footballer accused of murdering his wife and a male friend. After the Simpson trial, Dan Lungren, California's attorney general, complained about the 'oprahization' of American juries – a reference to the heated debates and instant verdicts of shows like the one hosted by Oprah Winfrey. 'Talk show watchers are widely considered by prosecutors and professional jury consultants to be more likely than others to distrust official accounts of "the truth",' Lungren said. Regrettable though this tendency, if true, may be from the point of view of an attorney general, it must be balanced against the possibility that trustworthiness of 'official accounts of truth' might indeed be legitimately doubted by black people. In the words of Kevin Glynn, an academic commentator, tabloid media 'multiplies and amplifies the heterogenous voices and viewpoints in circulation in contemporary culture, giving rein to many that are typically excluded from the dominant regime of truth through the dynamics of race, class, gender, age and sexuality.'

Catharine Lumby, an Australian journalist and academic, has gone further, arguing that talk shows like Winfrey's 'exemplify a new form of public speech, one which privileges experience over knowledge, emotion over reason, and popular opinion over expert advice.' She could have added that among the consequences of

14. Oprah Winfrey, the American talk-show host, has become a legendary figure in what some people call 'tabloid television', typically broadcast in the daytime and featuring live, studio based discussions with strong audience participation. According to critics, the 'oprah-ization' of American culture has involved diminished respect for authority, obsession with personal dramas, and 'dumped down' television. Oprah's supporters say she has been a key figure in democratizing American public life, giving a voice to people usually ignored by the media.

Winfrey's style, and her celebrity, was the development of the most successful book club in American literary history, as the television star in the late 1990s became the key driver of the country's best-seller lists. There are many instances of media celebrity being placed at the service of good causes, from the campaign against poverty in Africa led by rock stars Bob Geldof and Bono to the campaign for more nutritious school dinners promoted by the celebrity television chef Jamie Oliver in the run-up to the 2005 UK general election. David Kamp suggested in an article in *Vanity Fair* that 'the tabloidification of American life – of the news, of the

culture, yea, of human behaviour – is such a sweeping phenomenon that it can't be dismissed as merely a jokey footnote to the history of the 1990s. Rather, it's the very hallmark of our times; if the decade must have a name . . . it might as well be the Tabloid Decade.'

Tabloids and ambient news

Conducting focus groups with a very wide range of people in 2002, for a research project aimed at understanding the way people get news and how well they are served by it, I was struck again and again by the genuine hunger of people to understand issues, like the risks of certain vaccination programmes for their children, or the real patterns of crime in their neighbourhood. They are frustrated that no one is providing reliable information, in a way that is truly accessible.

These same people say that of all news media, they trust television as their main source. But this raises two difficulties. The first is that because television (and radio) news is free at the point of consumption and, essentially, ambient, younger people especially tend to believe that they will 'pick up' on anything important that is going on without needing to set out to find it, or to extend their circuits of information. They say that news is something which you follow when you are already aware something interesting is going on; a rational enough response in an era of ambient news, but one which risks narrowing information and news horizons. The second problem is that very little television news is truly local, which means that people feel decreasingly confident in their knowledge about what is going on in their own neighbourhoods. For many people in Britain today it is easier to find out what is going on in the Indian subcontinent or in American baseball than on the next street. The history of the internet, to date, suggests that this situation is being reinforced rather than reversed.

The real challenge raised by tabloid journalism is the extent to which it can widen people's genuine sense of engagement with the different worlds which affect their lives. The best tabloid journalism, which cuts through information clutter and speaks in plain language with strong emotional appeal, is likely to go on being highly valued in the more complex media environment into which we are moving.

Chapter 5

Up to a point, Lord Copper's: who owns journalists

Journalists are free-spirited individuals; mavericks not easily bound by corporate rule and regulation or, in certain situations, even by the law of the land. Yet almost all modern journalism takes place within a corporate setting, which limits and influences what journalists do. True, the internet, with its list-publishing, pod-casting, and web-log technology ('blogging') has again made it possible for journalists who lack access to a mainstream media outlet to publish their own work, but most journalists work for an organization or, if they are freelance, for a number of them. That is what A. J. Liebling had in mind when he remarked that freedom of the press exists only for those who happen to own one and that, in turn, is why the internet has been referred to as 'Liebling's revenge'. What effect do shifting forms of ownership and institutional setting have upon journalism?

It is important to clear up one misunderstanding. These days, in spite of the mythology, our news media are for the most part not run by press barons. The cigar-chomping tyrant who barks out orders for editorial lines, in between flogging ads and plotting the demise of some nearby president or prime minister, is largely a creature of the past, based on foundations built among the small printing shops of the pre-industrial era, when publishers literally wrote, printed, distributed, and sold advertisements for their newspapers. In the twenty-first century, we are shocked to see an anachronistic figure like the Canadian Lord Conrad Black, until recently owner of the *Daily Telegraph* and the *Jerusalem Post*, writing articles in his own titles. When, in the late 1980s, the doomed and dishonest press tycoon Robert Maxwell used the *Daily Mirror* to glorify himself on its front page, it was simply considered crass.

Corporate man cometh

So, if today's typical news media boss is not a Maxwell, Black, or even a Murdoch, what is he? He is most likely a professional manager, working in a corporate setting, and increasingly that corporate setting will entail involvement in a wide range of media, from the internet to movies, and be spread across many parts of the world. AOL–Time Warner is among the largest and most conspicuous of these multimedia beasts, being a fusion of the old Time Inc, Warner Brothers' film and music interests, and America Online, a pioneer of the commercial internet. AOL–Time Warner also owns several other large businesses, including Britain's IPC magazine group and CNN, the global television news service. In the same period that this empire was being assembled, Walt Disney snapped up ABC and Viacom bought CBS.

The desire for large companies to focus upon 'converged' media assets, however, will no doubt also turn out to be ephemeral. Only a couple of decades ago an entirely opposing fashion held sway. Then, diverse industrial conglomerates thought it was a good idea to own a few media assets, because the stock market admired diverse asset bases. This was the era which made NBC part of General Electric and CBS a sister company of Westinghouse. At that time Pearson, one of Britain's few players on the global media stage, combined interests ranging from investment banking, crockery and theme parks to the *Financial Times*, Penguin Books, and Australia's Grundy Television, producer of the soap opera *Neighbours*.

In global media terms, American companies are dominant simply because their domestic market is so much larger than any other and their language so widely spoken. They occupy roughly thirty slots in the list of the world's fifty largest media companies. The big non-American players include Germany's Bertelsmann, France's Vivendi, and Japan's Sony.

When press barons ruled the earth

But the myth of the hiring, firing, government-toppling press baron remains part of journalism's cultural heritage and it still informs the way journalists see themselves as buccaneering and hard driving heroes with dirty faces. No journalist working for a faceless global multinational company can fail to carry in his or her memory bank stories like the one immortalized in the semi-fictional persona of Citizen Kane, based on the life of William Randolph Hearst. In 1898, Hearst did more than anyone else to precipitate war between Spain and the United States. When the US battleship *Maine* sank in Havana Harbour, Hearst's papers falsely accused Spain of blowing it up and before the fighting began, dispatched an artist to illustrate reporters' dispatches. The illustrator, bored at the absence of death and destruction, cabled Hearst: 'Everything is quiet. There is no trouble here. There will be no war. I wish to return.' To which, Hearst's biographers record, the publisher replied: 'Please remain. You furnish pictures and I'll furnish war.' According to Hearst's son, this legendary reply was in fact never uttered – it is no doubt fitting that the most famous exchange in the history of newspapers was probably a fiction. That it *is* so well remembered owes everything to *Citizen Kane* where, his words sharpened by a Hollywood script writer, the boss declares: 'You provide the prose poems and I'll provide the war!'

In Britain, a wholly fictional figure captures the spirit of the press baron. Evelyn Waugh's comic masterpiece *Scoop* (1937) gave us Lord Copper, whose erratic judgement was surpassed only by the stridency with which it was delivered. Lord Copper's craven

15. William Randolph Hearst was the ultimate press baron, mixing politics, celebrity high life, and newspapering in a potent blend. Orson Welles based his film *Citizen Kane* on Hearst's life, but there is doubt about whether Hearst ever sent the famous message to one of his illustrators, telling him to stay in Cuba to cover a war that Hearst said he would ensure took place.

ORSON WELLES · JOSEPH COTTON in
"CITIZEN KANE"
A RITE RELEASE Cert A

underlings, trying like all good journalists to stay just on the right side of the truth, developed a standard reply to his peremptory formulations which echoes through newsrooms to this day: 'Up to a point, Lord Copper.'

All industrialized countries had their Lord Coppers. In France, the textile manufacturer Jean Prouvost built a press empire which included the daily *Le Figaro, Paris-Soir*, and two of the twentieth century's most successful magazines, *Marie-Claire* for women and the illustrated weekly news magazine *Paris-Match*. In Germany, Spain, and Italy, matters were complicated by the rise and fall of fascism. Germany's biggest media group today, Bertelsmann, has its roots in religious book publishing, but the country's dominant newspaper owner, Axel Springer, fits the Citizen Kane bill, even though his firm only began operations in Hamburg in 1946, under licence from the occupying British forces. Springer launched the populist *Bild-Zeitung* in 1952 and by the mid-1960s controlled 40 per cent of the West German press. Like Hearst, Springer is famed for a single pronouncement – that too much reflection is bad for Germans – and is also immortalized in a work of fiction, Heinrich Böll's *The Lost Honour of Katharina Blum*.

But gradually, the corporate types have overhauled the tycoons. Today, even the American supermarket tabloids, once the personal instrument of owner-publishers like Generoso Pope, are mostly small units in larger publishing groups, enjoying advantages of scale in back-office functions; cross-selling between different advertising markets and wielding greater weight in negotiations for publishing rights to celebrity content and sports rights.

It is a matter of heated debate which of these models best serves journalism. In the heyday of press barons, journalists had a great deal to say about their bosses' excesses, prejudices, vanity, and occasional brutality. Today, many journalists are critical of the power wielded by a Silvio Berlusconi or a Rupert Murdoch, who stand as exceptions to the decline of the media tycoon. Journalists, however, are not much enamoured of the press barons' 'corporate man' successors.

Profits of doom

The main current complaint is that the shareholder-owned company is too much focused upon quarter-to-quarter profits improvement. By incentivizing editors with share options and setting ambitious profits targets in response to Wall Street pressure, newspaper companies like Gannett and Knight Ridder are accused of distracting their editors from journalism's civic purpose and so damaging reader loyalty and the longer term health of the business. 'By the end of the twentieth century, in deed if not in name, America's journalistic leaders had been transformed into businesspeople. And half now report that they spend at least a third of their time on business matters rather than journalism,' argue leading lights in the influential Committee of Concerned Journalists.

Leonard Downie and Robert Kaiser, who work for an organization whose formal statement of mission declares a willingness to sacrifice profit for service to its readers (the *Washington Post*) have taken up this theme. Based on interviews with editors, past and present, across the United States, they accuse media corporations of demanding from their newsrooms soft features, friendly to local advertisers, and neglecting hard news. They illustrate the point with the example of one newspaper which, following its takeover by Gannett, started charging its readers lineage for obituaries of family members, rather than seeing these as independently reported news items. Everywhere, they find journalists' jobs and expenses cut, even when advertising is strong, and savagely so during revenue downturns. 'I'm worried about American journalism,' says one editor; 'as we lose the independents, I wonder who's going to watch the government.' Gannett, they say, regularly moves editors and publishers around 'so they are relative strangers in the communities they serve'. Jay Harris, who resigned as publisher of the *San Jose*

Mercury News, because his owners insisted upon cutting editorial expenses in order to boost already substantial profits, told fellow editors at a conference in 2001 that it was 'like watching a loved one commit suicide unintentionally'. In spite of all the smart new marketing techniques, and reader offers, sales of American newspapers fell throughout the 1990s and by 2000, only 55 per cent of American adults considered themselves regular newspaper readers, compared with 81 per cent in 1964.

Murdoch, last of the big beasts

How does this picture compare with, say, life on newspapers owned by one of the last great dynastic news barons? Rupert Murdoch has certainly invested, sometimes over-ambitiously, in newspapers and other news media. But he is pictured on the front of the most widely used media studies textbook in Britain armed with a knife and fork as he prepares to carve up a vulnerable planet earth. This reflects the widespread view that Murdoch has over-used his political influence to support his business goals on three continents, not least by opposing the growth in influence of the European Union, an issue on which his UK newspapers have been single-minded over the years. Yet, as Colin Seymour-Ure has pointed out, the 35 per cent share of the UK national newspaper market held by Murdoch's News International at the start of the twenty-first century was smaller than the proportion controlled by Lord Harmsworth a hundred years earlier. And during that same century, the BBC was constructed from scratch, and built for itself a 40 per cent share of the UK radio and television market – a level the competition authorities would never countenance for a private owner.

Murdoch, however, appears content to play the bogeyman; perhaps it is the mischief-making journalist in him. When he arrived in Britain to take over the *News of the World* in 1969, he was asked whether he would interfere in the editorial operation. He hadn't, he replied, come from the other side of the world merely to sit back and watch. Murdoch demonology has him firing editors like a bored

16. Rupert Murdoch, last of the great press barons. In 1993, Murdoch said the days of the press magnate were gone, replaced by a 'bevy of harassed and sometimes confused media executives, trying to guess at what the public wants'.

youth spitting out watermelon seeds and it is true that he has removed talented people who stood in his way, including the respected Harold Evans, who quit the editor's chair at *The Times* live on the Britain's main evening television news in 1983. But it is not true to say that Murdoch has routinely operated a revolving door for editors at any of his newspapers. As he explained himself in an interview in 1999: 'If an editor is producing a paper you are basically pleased with and proud of . . . then he is very safe in his job. If an editor is producing a paper which is clearly failing, turning the community against it, then you have to make changes. I've been in that position once or twice and been criticised for being ruthless in changing editors, but the people who'll be ruthless are the shareholders, who'll get rid of me if the papers go bust.'

No one much believed Murdoch when, in a speech in London in 1993, he announced that the day of the media mogul was done, but he was, more or less, right. 'The days when a few newspaper publishers could sit down and agree to keep an entire nation ignorant of a major event are long gone,' he said. 'Technology is racing ahead so rapidly, news and entertainment sources are proliferating at such a rate, that the media mogul has been replaced by a bevy of harassed and sometimes confused media executives, trying to guess at what the public wants.'

'These people are not journalists'

The truth is that it is difficult to generalize about the ownership conditions that make a great newspaper possible. Tom Rosenstiel of the Committee of Concerned Journalists insists that 'the biggest change is that most journalism is no longer produced primarily by companies engaged mostly in journalism.' An example is Time Inc, which once garnered all of its revenues from journalism. When Time Inc merged with Warner Communications, about 50 per cent of its revenues came from journalism. With the merger between Time Warner and AOL, journalism accounted for less than five per cent of revenues, even though the company still controlled 35 per cent of all the magazine circulation in the United States. 'So a major part of magazine journalism in the US is a tiny part of this giant conglomerate,' says Rosenstiel: 'The values of the people who run that company are very different. These are not journalists in the sense that Henry Luce (*Time*'s founder) was.'

Yet journalism does not always prosper inside family-owned companies, which often run out of willpower and capital. And there are, undeniably, great newspapers owned by public companies, among them the *Wall Street Journal* and the *New York Times*. Equally, there are world-class papers owned by families or trusts (the *Guardian* and the *Washington Post*), just as there are truly excellent news organizations, like the BBC, within the public sector, though it's also true to say there are also many terrible ones, including most of the world's state broadcasters. The simple test of what type of organization owns a news outlet doesn't really tell you much about how its journalism will prosper.

Newspapers in trouble

Many of the problems attributed to 'bad' owners are probably, in reality, more due to the fact that newspapers everywhere are struggling to maintain circulation and share of advertising revenues against growing electronic competition. Although newspapers will be with us for a long time to come, television and radio have eaten away at their display advertising and new electronic media have dealt two further blows: siphoning off some classified job, property, and car advertising and extending the unhelpful practice of making news free at the point of the consumption, which undermines newspaper cover prices.

These pressures follow decades when a lot of newspaper businesses were not at all well run. In Britain's overcrowded national newspaper market, chaotic labour relations were a fact of life for many years and any cash generated during the good years was squandered in subsequent price wars or uneconomic addition of new sections. In the regional press, sales of daily newspapers continued to fall sharply in the 1990s, encouraging steady consolidation into larger groups. Between 1945 and 1995, the number of morning titles published outside London fell by a third and the survivors struggled to hold circulation. Just as American cities became one-newspaper towns, in this period cities that had enjoyed the services of two evening newspapers were reduced to a single title, though the total number of provincial evening newspapers fell only slightly, to sixty-eight. Weekly local papers have fared better, though they too have been hurt by the growth in free newspapers. Among the bottom line effects: fewer editorial resources and declining relative pay for journalists.

In the world of broadcast journalism, the emergence of the pan-media conglomerate has also raised concerns that news organizations once trusted for their impartiality are tainted by their association with entertainment. So, if an American network broadcaster uses its news programmes to give uncritical coverage of, say, its latest movie blockbuster, it damages the trust in its news operation. Occasionally, these conflicts of interests by media owners have developed into full-blown scandal, as when CBS was shown to have pulled its punches on a current affairs investigation into smoking and health, at a time when its owner was negotiating a takeover deal in the tobacco industry. This blunder eventually got the full Hollywood treatment in Michael Mann's 1999 film, *The Insider*, starring Al Pacino and Russell Crowe.

Ownership: myth and reality

Because the mass media are a source of power, their ownership (whatever form it takes) will always bring temptations to abuse of influence. That being so, it is wise to try to ensure that no society depends too heavily upon a narrow range of owners, which in turn underlines the need for national and international laws to limit concentration of media ownership. Today, there is much talk about the emergence of an unprecedented global oligopoly, operating in media markets all over the world, and capable of dominating markets for distribution and content rights.

It is not yet clear that this alarm is justified. The most comprehensive study of the situation in the United States, for example, showed that there had been 'only modest shifts in the role of major players in the media industry between 1980 and 1998'. This is, in part, because laws which resist media concentration have caused firms to dispose of some interests, as they acquire new ones. That pressure to re-fragment after consolidation may also partly explain why only a third of the companies that made the list in 1980 were still players in 1998. From this, you might conclude that the most salient characteristic of modern media ownership is not its concentration, but its instability. The authors of the study referred to conclude that the US media industry is 'one of the most competitive major industries in the US'. They go on to say that 'in the world of unlimited virtual bandwidth, the curse of who owns the media may be in its unwieldy anarchy rather than in the feared controlled oligopoly'. Even News Corporation's buying up of local television stations in the US, a notorious act of media concentration, enabled Fox to create a fourth television network, creating greater competition for ABC, CBS, and NBC.

That said, the desire to resist excessive media concentration remains a lively and proper political concern in most countries, on the grounds that plurality of ownership is more likely to lead to diversity of editorial approach.

In practice, methods to resist media concentration take many different forms. In Scandinavia, governments provide subsidies to newspapers threatened with closure where the result would be monopoly publishing. The US Congress, in 1970, passed the Newspaper Preservation Act, designed to check the economic forces leading to the closure of second newspapers in American towns and cities. One of its measures involved allowing rival companies to share plant and other overheads, so long as they preserved titles under separate ownership and editorial control. The law's impact, however, was less marked than its advocates hoped. By the late

1990s, only thirty-four cities had two newspapers, compared with more than 500 in the 1920s.

This rapid consolidation was to some extent counterbalanced by the very rapid growth in other media, such as magazines. Between 1950 and 1998, the number of magazine titles in the US almost doubled, from 6,600 to 11,800. Concerns about diminished plurality of ownership also must be set alongside the growth in electronic media. In Britain, in the last decade, the number of commercial radio stations has grown from 50 to 250 and television offers more than 200 channels, compared with four or five a decade ago. Most of these broadcast media offer some sort of news service, with the result that the total volume of television news on offer to British viewers in multi-channel homes increased roughly eightfold during the 1990s. Behind this proliferation of news, however, there are still significant news gaps. British television, for example, has so far failed to achieve significant provision of local news services and most of the growth in commercial radio has been in music services whose level of interest in news and political affairs was demonstrated during the 2001 general election, when only a dozen stations chose to involve their listeners in a a live phone-in with Tony Blair, the prime minister, and his rivals for office.

Do journalists care who they work for?

It is clear then that there are many good political, economic and cultural reasons to care about who owns the institutions from which we get our journalism. But what do the journalists themselves think? The answer is that they are inclined to grumble a lot, whoever is boss. This explains why, despite countless attempts, journalists have not been good at forming powerful professional associations to regulate their own professional standards or even, in most countries, at running effective trade unions.

Having worked myself for a British shareholder-owned company (Pearson); a publicly owned corporation (the BBC); a proprietor-owned magazine (the *New Statesman*) and a newspaper owned by a mixture of British, Irish, Italian, and Spanish shareholders (the *Independent*), I could not say that one 'model' is preferable to another. Outstanding journalism was done in all these settings and each had its weaknesses. At the BBC, there was a sense of a great tradition of public service, and genuine concern at every level for accuracy and fairness, but there was also hefty bureaucracy and a culture which militated against risk-taking. You would not want all your journalism produced by an institution like the BBC: it would be too cautious. Working for the *Financial Times*, the atmosphere was intellectually bracing and wonderfully international. But it could also be deadeningly narrow. Every year, we had a competition for the dullest headline on the paper and there was never a shortage of entries. For some reason, it is a line about unchanged levels of anchovy catches off the Peruvian coast which has stuck in my memory. The *Financial Times*, at its worst, is capable of reducing a cataclysm on any scale to its effect upon world stock markets.

The editor's life

After fifteen years at the *FT*, I became editor of the *Independent* during a period of the purest madness, when the paper was lurching from widely held ownership towards a more secure resting place in Tony O'Reilly's Dublin-based Independent group. By the time I got to the paper in 1994, Rupert Murdoch had launched a price war designed to kill us off, at a time when the *Independent* was managed by ex-Murdoch executives from the Caligula school of management. They were themselves constantly plotting against the other shareholders, but still had the power to order me to cut the editorial budget by a third, and then, as soon as I had done so, by almost the same amount again, at which point I declined and was relieved of my duties. Somehow, in the middle of it all, writers continued to produce great pieces, to which readers reacted with a readerly blend of enthusiasm, puzzlement and outrage. In the late afternoon of a particularly bloody day I shut the door of my office, looking west from the Canary Wharf tower, and wrote an editorial parodying a Shakespeare play. I can't now remember its subject, or even the name of the play, but the letter I got from a reader saying that it was reassuring to know the paper's sense of humour and style was in such sound health stands out as a high point in a tough period.

The *New Statesman* also involved close contact with readers, many of whom worked in or around Parliament and so within a mile of the magazine's offices. Our entire editorial team at the *Statesman* never exceeded eight, which meant the editor had to do a great deal of coaxing to get good writers to contribute to the magazine at a fraction of their normal rates of pay. What an editor needs to do the job well is enough money to hire writers, reporters, editors, graphic artists, and photographers; freedom to take editorial decisions and as much managerial stability and support as possible. The task often seemed to me to be comparable to that of managing a football club: exciting, turbulent, and hugely rewarding when things are going your way. If you lose the support of your boss, be that owner, chief executive, or chairman, there is no point debating the rights and wrongs. 'It's only a question of when, not if, you get the boot,' Kelvin Mackenzie, the former *Sun* editor, told me in the back of a taxi one day during my tenure at the *Independent*. When a strong, inventive editor happens to coincide with stable ownership and shrewd business management, great things are possible. But these conditions can arrive, or not, in any system of ownership. Utopian forms of worker control do not achieve much if the advertising department cannot sell space. What readers, viewers, and listeners need is a diversity of models, along with a diversity of owners. France's *Le Monde*, for example, is one-third owned by its journalists. Shareholder-owned and proprietor-owned news media are fine in the mix, so long as they do not drive out all the alternatives. It does matter who owns journalists, but it is not the only thing that matters: journalism, if it is any good, is chiefly concerned with the world beyond itself.

That does not mean that journalists or their editors should be unreflective about the business settings in which they work. Adam Michnik, editor-in-chief of *Gazeta Wyborcza*, refused to accept share options in what became an increasingly powerful publishing group in post-cold war Poland on the grounds that, as editor, he felt he should measure himself not by the growth in shareholder value, but by the service provided to readers. Agora, the company which owns the newspaper, also set up a charitable trust to hold 7.5 per cent of its stock when it was successfully floated on the stock market in 1999. 'This isn't just a business for us,' said Wanda Rapaczynski, chief executive of Agora; 'part of being a free media, untainted by political interests, is being willing to play a role in the country's democracy. And part of that belief is being committed to broad ownership of this company and giving back to our country.' Does Agora offer a model? Possibly not. But an admirable example? Certainly.

Editors and their owners do also, sometimes, face intractable difficulties. When, in 1996, I went to edit the *New Statesman*, it had just been bought by Geoffrey Robinson, a businessman and Labour Member of Parliament. Robinson was an ideal owner in that he invested generously in the business and kept out of editorial decisions. On one occasion, Clare Short, an outspoken figure in Tony Blair's shadow ministerial team, gave us an interview in which she attacked her boss's spin doctors as the 'people in the dark'. After going to press, I phoned Robinson to warn him of the row that would soon engulf the magazine. He was on holiday in Kenya. Having heard an account of the interview he replied: 'From where I am standing, I can see a lioness approaching. It's really quite remarkable here.' It was the end of the conversation. Later, during his time as Treasury minister, Robinson's own business affairs were the subject of official investigation. What should the *New Statesman* do? Pile in with its own investigations? Defend him or give him space to defend himself? I felt we would not be trusted if we took either course, so we explained to our readers that this was a story we would leave to others. A previous *New Statesman* editor was in print

with a fierce denunciation of me in the next edition of the
Guardian.

Editors count on their owners at moments of crisis. As editor of the
Independent, I was prosecuted following a decision to publish
leaked material from a court case, which revealed government
duplicity in the overseas sale of armaments. If we lost, the lawyers
said, I could go to jail. In the end, we won the case. Curiously
enough, I never doubted for a moment that the *Independent*'s
management, with whom I was not on the best of terms, would
stand by me at this difficult moment. That says a great deal about
the bond between journalists and owners when they face the test of
whether they're prepared to take risks to hold power to account.

Chapter 6

Hacks v. flaks: journalism and public relations

Of the many self-indulging aphorisms beloved of journalists, one of the most comforting states: 'News is something somebody somewhere doesn't want printed. All the rest is advertising.' Sometimes attributed to Lord Northcliffe, the British press baron, it is easy to see why this breezy over-simplification exerts such appeal, portraying the journalist as crusader, single-mindedly engaged in exposing truth against the odds. The quotation pops up all over the place: it was even taken as a mission statement by a technology news website to contrast the value of its own information, paid for by reader subscription, with news tainted by association with public relations people, advertisers, or sponsors.

The Northcliffe doctrine raises one of the central issues in journalism, namely, in whose interests does the journalist work: for the company or organization which employs him or for a wider public good? And if journalists in a commercial setting are primarily working for shareholder profits, or the esteem of their own organization, can they legitimately draw such a sharp distinction between the value and plausibility of their own work and other forms of professional communications, namely the information put out to the public directly by organizations through their own channels?

The more that journalism resembles mere entertainment,

brokering paid for messages into the public domain, the harder this question bites and the more difficult it becomes to defend or advance the privileges democratic societies afford journalists such as the qualified right not to reveal sources of information; and the right, subject to laws of libel and contempt, to free expression. The Northcliffe doctrine cheerily evades such complexities. According to it, news cannot come from PR men. It must be hard-won. As the journalist Claud Cockburn once said: 'Never believe anything until it is officially denied.'

Mau-mau the flak-catchers

Tom Wolfe captured the spirit of the matter in his report of life in San Francisco's anti-poverty programme in 1970. Wolfe's portrait of the shifty 'flak-catcher' portrays the official spokesman with nothing at his disposal but hollow words, confronted or 'mau-maued' by an angry group demanding to know why their subsidized job scheme is to be cut back. Wolfe writes:

'This lifer is ready to catch whatever flak you're sending up. It doesn't matter what bureau they put him in. It's all the same. Poverty, Japanese imports, valley fever, tomato-crop parity, partial disability, home loans, second-probate accounting, the Interstate 90 detour change order, lockouts, secondary boycotts, GI alimony, the Pakistani quota, cinch mites, Tularemic Loa loa, veterans' dental benefits, workmen's compensation, suspended excise rebates – whatever you're angry about, it doesn't matter, he's there to catch the flak. He's a lifer.'

The uncomfortable fact for journalists today, one hundred years since the birth of the public relations industry, is that there are in the United States more flak-catchers (or 'flaks' as reporters sometimes call them) than journalists (or hacks, as journalists sometimes call themselves). And where the US leads in such matters, others tend to follow. Nor do today's flak-catchers merely or mainly block the hacks' flak: they pre-empt it and get the journalists, wherever they can, to see matters their way. The fear among journalists is that they no longer have the resources to counter the increasingly sophisticated munitions of their traditional enemy. Journalism, they fear, is being hung out to dry by the not-so-hidden persuaders.

It is true that public relations people, especially those working in the upper reaches of financial, corporate, and government public relations, are better paid than all but a handful of very senior or celebrity journalists; they also frequently have access to better technology and support systems. Some would say, but this is more controversial, that they are also better disciplined, more professional, and more skilful, and that this is the main reason journalism is in danger of being outsmarted. 'The trouble with journalism today,' one senior public relations executive told me, 'is that the journalists we deal with tend to be rather young, not very experienced and stretched by the number of deadlines they're running against. You often feel that you are dealing with people who really don't understand the story. That's quite scary.' Anyone who has been on the receiving end of a journalist's enquiries will recognize an element of truth in this: there is nothing quite so terrifying as the knowledge that someone is about to tell a few million people about yourself or your organization without understanding it or, sometimes, even taking the trouble to try. In such circumstances a reporter's well-informed scepticism, even prejudiced hostility, is greatly to be preferred to ignorance and laziness.

Journalists are also less than honest when they pretend that they do not make use of public relations contacts and other official sources of information. They will want to swagger, with Claud Cockburn, but in reality, journalists use any source of information they can tap. A journalist covering any beat naturally wants access to top people: the decision takers and primary sources. But this is not always realistic: top people are, by definition, too busy to spend all day on the phone to journalists, so they surround themselves with intermediaries, whose job it is to deal with the news media that operate around the clock, around the year. Skilled reporters recognize that there is a hierarchy of sources for information and that you don't go to your top contacts for routine facts, or to check history.

Lazy journalism

But lazy journalists and thinly resourced newspapers, trade magazines, or broadcast newsrooms do become overdependent upon these intermediaries, often reproducing gratefully whatever ready-made material comes their way. The too quickly sub-edited press release, or even the non-edited version, can be inspected any day in thousands of publications. Free newspapers and smaller commercial radio stations often operate with few or even no reporters, publishing only what someone sends in. As long ago as the 1950s, Scott Cutlip attempted to calculate the proportion of American news column inches taken up with information supplied by public relations practitioners. His conclusion was that nearly half of what we read came via this route. And that was before the dramatic increase in the scale of US public relations industry in the last forty years of the century, and the corresponding decline in editorial resources on many newspapers. No wonder the information we get from the news media is so often so uniform and repetitive.

Today, public relations professionals hand out not only press releases, but photographs, CD-ROM images, audio and video clips. The top PR firms video their clients' public events and webcast them, to be picked up by journalists, or for direct consumption by interested parties, underlining another way in which the internet makes it even harder to distinguish journalism from other forms of what is sometimes called 'commercial speech.' There was controversy in the 1980s when the BBC broadcast video supplied by the environmental campaign group Greenpeace, on the grounds that it was not 'independent' material. Today, broadcasters frequently use video material supplied by a huge range of sources, including members of the public, millions of whom can now shoot and transmit video on their mobile phones. Organizations like Greenpeace see their media strategy as offering to supporters and other interested parties what is in effect an authored, on-line service of broadcast information and pictures. Even the British royal family has a series of websites, which are used to rebut what they regard as misleading reports in the newspapers.

With web-sites, at least you can usually identify the commercial or other interests involved. With the mainstream mass media this is not always the case. Commercial product placement in movies and television programmes is designed to promote consumer products in a subtle or hidden way, and in many newspapers and magazines you will see 'advertorials' commissioned only because they have the support of specific advertisers or sponsors. Is this really journalism assembled without fear or favour? The truth is that some advertorials are more honest and honourable than others but many are a disgrace.

Enter the spin doctor

The growth of public relations has caused particular concern in the field of politics, with the emergence of the political 'spin-doctor' in American politics in the 1980s and since then almost everywhere else. Politicians tend to blame the media for this phenomenon, which they see as a response to news media which no longer separate fact and comment and in effect 'spin' against the politicians, provoking a response in kind. Whoever is to blame, these practices are widely blamed for undermining the reputation of politicians for plain speaking and even for the decline in public participation in elections. One spin-doctor in Tony Blair's government was forced to resign when it was revealed that she had sent an email on the day of the terrorist attacks on New York and Washington in September 2001, pointing out that this would be a good day 'to bury some bad news' about local government expenditure.

Politics, however, is not the only area where the activities of journalists and public relations collide. In business and financial markets, unscrupulous public relations professionals circulate information, often false or half-false and designed to raise the stock price of companies for which they work, a task which involves collusion with investment bankers, stock analysts and others who straddle the line between investment advice, salesmanship, and journalism. Since the collapse of stock markets in 2001/2, these practices have attracted the attention of financial market regulators around the world, some of whom have moved to make rules which require journalists and other media players to identify their financial interests when pontificating in print or on air. 'The world of Wall Street spin is . . . a daily, dizzying match in which stock prices, corporate earnings, and millions of individual investments are riding on the outcome', says Howard Kurtz, media reporter for the *Washington Post*. 'In this overheated environment, the degree to which basic facts can be massaged, manipulated, and hyped is truly troubling. And that raises the fundamental question: amid the endless noise, whom do you trust?'

Whom indeed. From whichever direction you approach the intertwined worlds of journalism and public relations, trust is the critical issue. Should the public's working assumption be that any unmediated message, from a politician, government department, non-governmental organization, or business is either a lie or self-serving half-truth, the impression often given by journalists? If so, can they make the assumption that journalists have the integrity to test and interrogate rival claims, serving a general public interest? Given the low level of trust the public has in journalists, some modesty is in order. It helps to understand today's tensions between journalism and public relations to understand something of their interconnected history.

How journalists created the PR industry

The first recognizable public relations agency was born in Boston in 1900, but the idea of 'persuasive speech' is at least as old as Plato. The word propaganda has its origin in the seventeenth-century Roman Catholic Church's 'Congregatio de Propaganda Fide', literally aimed at propagating the faith. Public relations as we know it emerged as an aspect of modern industrial management in the early 1900s as the United States engaged in one of its periodic backlashes against excessive business power. This was the age of the trust-busters, who broke up business empires in the Rockefeller era. Soon, every self-respecting business had a team of lawyers to deal with the competition authorities and professional communicators to promote its cause with journalists and the public. The obvious place to recruit these communicators was from newspapers.

William Wolff Smith was still a reporter for the *Baltimore Sun* when he opened his 'publicity business' in Washington in 1902 and he continued to operate as a 'stringer' or part-time correspondent for a number of newspapers, while supplying pieces reflecting the views and interests of his clients. Rockefeller's first public relations 'counsellor' was Ivy Ledbetter Lee, son of a Methodist preacher from Georgia, and a former police reporter on Hearst's *New York Journal*. Lee joined the Rockefeller payroll in 1914, following his skilful work in handling the aftermath of the company's bloody assault against striking Colorado mine-workers and their families (the 'Ludlow Massacre'). One of the radical journalists who reported the massacre, George Creel, went on to make his own name in another branch of public relations, chairing the path-breaking Committee on Public Information, which sought to unite public opinion at home and propagandize on behalf of the United States abroad during the First World War. After the Armistice, Creel's vast programme released into the American private sector a demobbed army of public relations experts, who built the modern public relations industry. Edward Bernays, a sometime reporter and Broadway theatrical press agent, worked for the Creel committee, before starting his own agency in 1919, in partnership with his wife.

Engineering consent

Lee was clear that, for his techniques to succeed, his clients must show integrity in order to win trust. Only honest companies would meet 'the high demands of enlightened public sentiment'. Others took their calling even more seriously. Walter Lippman's seminal book *Public Opinion* (1922) recommended the application of social scientific techniques to the measurement and shaping of public attitudes. Meanwhile Bernays, nephew of the psychologist Sigmund Freud, set out out the novel idea that public relations was a two-way affair, which involved the professional PR 'counsel' shaping the behaviour of the client, as well as the attitude of the public. Bernays' statement of 'philosophy' remains a classic text in public communications:

> 'The counsel directs and supervises the activities of his clients wherever they impinge upon the daily life of the public. He interprets the client to the public and he interprets the public to the client. Perhaps the chief contribution of the public relations counsel to the public and to his client is his ability to understand and analyse obscure tendencies of the public mind. He first analyses his client's problem – he then analyzes the public mind.'

It was a short step from Bernays's pioneering thoughts to his concept of 'engineering consent' for an organization's goals. To some, this sounded too much like hypnosis and propaganda. They argued that the public relations practitioner had 'an ethical duty above that of his clients to the larger society'. Barely out of its infancy, public relations was caught in a moral dialogue closely resembling the one still taking place today in journalism.

These loftier notions have, of course, encountered very many practical difficulties, as one PR firm or another has snatched at the cash, rather than pausing to ask any sort of ethical question. Ivy Lee's career ended in shame when it turned out he was a paid adviser to I. G. Farben, the German chemical giant which assisted in Hitler's attempted extermination of the Jews.

Fakes and other mistakes

Not quite on the same scale, but probably more morally devious, were Hill and Knowlton's actions in the war which followed the invasion of Kuwait by Iraq in 1990. Employed by the Kuwaiti monarchy at a fee of $12 million to promote its interests inside the United States, the firm established a front organization called Citizens for a Free Kuwait. This, in turn, proceeded to manufacture stories about Iraqi atrocities in Kuwait. Nayriah, a sobbing 15-year-old girl, testified to a public hearing of Congress's Human Rights Caucus on 10 October 1990. She reported that she had seen Iraqi soldiers taking babies out of hospital incubators and leaving them 'to die on the cold floor'. Shortly afterwards, she was unmasked as the Washington-based daughter of the Kuwaiti ambassador. Hill and Knowlton also spent years conveying the tobacco industry's case that its products were not to blame for lung cancer and other diseases. It was perhaps out of such hard-bitten experience that John Hill, one of the firm's founders, advanced a less morally high-flown definition of the goals of public relations as: 'the management function which gives the same organized and careful attention to the asset of good will as is given to any other major asset of the business.'

Politics and PR

But it was in the sphere of politics that public relations became most controversial. Hamilton Wright, whose early career included a spell on the *Los Angeles Times*, built the first public relations organization devoted to promoting the interests of overseas countries. One of his techniques was to make a contractual guarantee to his clients that the money they paid him would buy at least five times as much publicity as the equivalent amount spent on advertising. Much later, in 1964, the Public Relations Society of America censured the firm, by then run by Wright's grandson, for violating one of its articles, which forbade pledging 'the achievement of specified results beyond a member's direct control'. But the accused man simply quit the society and carried on business as usual, illustrating another similarity between public relations and newspaper journalism: its resistance to any form of truly independent regulation.

More momentous was the work in 1930s California of two ex-reporters, the husband and wife team of Clem Whitaker and Leone Baxter, who came together to fight and win a local referendum. Flushed with this success, they formed Campaigns Inc, the first professional campaign consultants, a breed which has dominated every American election campaign since. In Whitaker's own words, they transformed campaign management from being 'a hit or miss business, directed by broken-down politicians' to being 'a mature, well-managed business founded on sound public relations principles, and using every technique of modern advertising'.

Bill and Tony go large

The vigour of their legacy is today evident all over the world, not least in the rise of Bill Clinton to the presidency of the United States and the modernization of the British Labour Party under Tony Blair, which in turn influenced Gerhard Schröder's leadership of the German Social Democratic Party (SPD) and Lionel Jospin's Socialist Party in the late 1990s. Philip Gould, a senior communications adviser to Tony Blair, has written extensively about the lessons 'New Labour' learnt from Clinton's New Democrats. He recalls a visit to Clinton's base in Arkansas in 1992 which proved a 'turning point . . . which gave me the will to go on' as the New Democrats displayed their deployment of a highly disciplined set of communications techniques, most of them learnt from business public relations and marketing, including sophisticated data management to track voter opinions, identify possible switchers and ensure instant rebuttal of hostile points. From this point on, New Labour became famous for the centralized running of its campaigns from a single 'war room' and the insistence that everyone involved in the campaign and beyond should be 'on message' at all times, so that key lines could be repeated time and again without self-contradiction.

Any journalist exposed to the New Democrats' or New Labour's methods can testify to their zeal. A few weeks before the May 1997 general election, I was editing the *New Statesman*, a political magazine which had developed a reputation for springing stories picked up by other news media. One day, just before dispatching the final pages to the printer, I took a telephone call from the Labour Party's headquarters, to be told: 'I'm calling from the Rapid Rebuttal unit. Could you tell me what you are putting in the magazine this week, so that I can prepare a rebuttal?' Gould denies that there is anything exceptional or morally dubious about the techniques of 'spin' with which New Labour became deeply associated. According to Gould, spin is 'a longstanding and completely unexceptional activity. In a world in which political parties, and other high-profile organizations, are under twenty-four hour media attack, it is common sense to employ people to put the view of the party or the organization and to do it to best effect. In a modern media environment, competence and good communications are inseparable: you cannot have one without the other.'

Gould is certainly right that Ivy Lee and John Hill were spin-doctors before Tony Blair was born. But these early public relations figures were operating in a world where the news media were less powerful and certainly less ubiquitous. Today, political life often appears to be a media phenomenon itself, as politicians dash from studio to studio, spending more time on television than they do in their parliaments or Cabinet meetings. Piers Morgan, who edited the Daily Mirror during part of the Blair premiership, has revealed

17. In the 1990s President Bill Clinton invented and led the 'New Democrats' and Blair led 'New Labour'. Both perfected techniques of political communication ('spin') and other campaign methods which built upon techniques used in commercial public relations. By the turn of the century, these methods were controversial and, some said, counterproductive.

that in a period of about nine years, he lunched or dined with the Prime Minister on no fewer than 18 occasions and met him a further 30 times for private chats or interviews. In modern politics, it does often seem that, as Marshall McLuhan foresaw, the medium has become the message, that 'the new media are not bridges between man and nature; they are nature'. From the point of view of anyone seriously engaged in trying to deliver effective government, the effect of spin, combined with changes in journalistic standards and cultures, has become debilitating. In the words of Geoff Mulgan, who spent seven years at the helm of Prime Minister Blair's policy strategy group, the gap between public perception and reality has become so large that it 'promotes the idea that there are no truths, only strategies and claims.' Many British and American journalists certainly felt that the spin-doctors they dealt with in the 1990s had taken them into a new territory of evasion, manipulation and deceit. The fact that Blair, by the time of his second landslide victory in 2001, was busily attempting to distance himself from the charge that his was a government of 'spin not substance' indicated that he was starting to understand the price paid for his earlier public relations triumph.

Money makes the spin go round

The role of spin in the world of business and financial markets has much in common with its political manifestation, except that here the fall-out has included collapsed share prices, corporate crisis and lost jobs. During the extraordinary period between 1997 and 2001, when the 'dot com boom' drove share prices to unprecedented heights, business journalism was itself being transformed by the growth of a new generation of specialist television channels and a profusion of web-based business services which delivered multiple streams of global data and pictures to traders' desks simultaneously all over the planet. By the turn of the century, a venerable firm like the news agency Reuters had been reinvented as a supplier of multimedia electronic market information to business and financial organizations. Amid this gold-rush, those who reported and commented on the market and individual stocks, whether live on television or via the web, were seldom asked to disclose their own financial interests, though informed insiders know full well that the expert Wall Street and City of London analysts employed by investment banks routinely issue nine 'buy' recommendations for every 'sell'.

One of the more extraordinary figures of this period was James Cramer, a millionaire Wall Street trader who combined the running of his own hedge fund for investors with a large stake in, and regular editorial appearances on, thestreet.com, an online news service in which the *New York Times* bought shares. Although it was editorial policy on thestreet.com for Cramer to declare his personal or professional interest in any stock mentioned in his commentaries, there were huge tensions in play. Was it legitimate for someone to be both a major private investor and a journalist serving his readers and viewers? In the same bull market, editorial dishonesty surfaced in more traditional news organizations. Journalists from the *Daily Mirror* in London and the *San Jose Mercury News* in the United States were caught lining their own pockets using information gathered in the course of their journalistic activities. Many expected the editor of the *Daily Mirror*, Piers Morgan, who had traded stock on the basis of his city desk's inside tips, to be fired, but he retained the support of the company, until eventually a bigger, political scandal forced him from office.

But Morgan's was not the only apologia as sobriety returned to Wall Street. Richard Lambert, editor of the *Financial Times* throughout the 1990s, acknowledged the failures of even the best business journalists in the world to spot the dubious business practices that started to come to light when the boom turned to crash at firms like Enron and Worldcom. 'The Enron affair reveals something about the culture of business journalism. As editor of the *Financial Times* over the period, I was part of the culture,' says Lambert. He notes that the signs of Enron's impending difficulties were, from the vantage point of the company's crash, 'there for anyone who cared to look'. Why did business journalists fail to spot them? 'Because they were too influenced by the views of big financial institutions, many of which rated Enron a 'buy' to the bitter end; because too much business journalism today is concerned with personalities rather than hard analysis and because business, unlike politics, is largely conducted without transparency and behind the protection of fierce libel laws, especially in Britain. 'One of the main tasks of the media is to hold power to account. With no serious alternative to free market capitalism, governments are increasingly obliged to enter into relationships with corporations. An intelligent examination of business starts to become a crucial component of democratic choice.' Lambert's words remind me of a story from the earliest days of the *Financial Times*, when its young chairman, Horatio Bottomley, found himself stitching mail bags in jail, following his involvement in a mining industry scam. A visitor sighed: 'Ah, Bottomley, sewing?' to which the disgraced publisher replied: 'No, reaping.'

Trust bust

There is an echo here with the world of political spin. In Philip Gould's own account of the rise of Tony Blair's New Labour, he turns to David Hill for a description of the spin-doctor's work. Hill, for many years the Labour Party's chief media spokesman and a bridge between the worlds of 'old' and 'new' Labour, spent a period in commercial public relations before returning to Downing Street as the Prime Minister's spokesman, following the resignation of the arch-spin doctor, Alastair Campbell. This is what Hill told Gould: 'You have to never tell a lie – telling lies is disastrous, because one of the most effective elements in being a spin-doctor is that they believe what you are saying to them.'

It is this erosion of trust that has spread a cynical rot through politics and business. Deterioration in standards of professional behaviour by journalists, public relations people and politicians have all contributed to this state of affairs. Public relations and journalism have different jobs to do in that journalists serve first and foremost the collective interest of their readers, viewers and listeners, before they serve the interests of the organizations which employ them, whereas PR people are employed explicitly to serve the interests of the organizations which pay their salaries. But without trust between them, politicians, business people, journalists, and public relations practitioners will not be trusted by the public, which means that none of them can do their jobs effectively. These people all depend upon trust in public communications. They are in the same boat and they would row to better effect if they acknowledged the fact, before then doing battle.

Chapter 7
Murder is my meat: the ethics of journalism

Journalism is a domain of moral choices, occasionally involving a melodramatic interplay between good and evil, which probably explains why the news media have proved such a fertile source of movie story-lines. According to one authority, Hollywood alone has churned out more than a thousand films which are, in one way or another, about the news business and its ethical challenges.

These celluloid heroes have come in many shapes and sizes, reflecting the concerns of their day. In the 1930s, Torchy Blane, a female reporter, tested gender stereotypes in the urban jungle, demanding entry to a crime scene with the words: 'Holdups and murders are my meat. I'm Torchy Blane of the Star.' Orson Welles's *Citizen Kane*, based upon the career of William Randolph Hearst, explored his subject's inability to discern the difference between fact and fiction. 'He was disappointed in the world, so he built one of his own,' says one of Kane's aides. This same decade also yielded the first of four screen adaptations of a Broadway play, *The Front Page* (1931), featuring Hildy Johnson's irrefutable description of the general news reporter's life: 'It's peeking through keyholes. It's running after fire engines, waking up people in the middle of the night. It's stealing pictures off little old ladies after their daughters get attacked.' In *Five Star Final* (1931) Edward G. Robinson's rag delights in ruining the lives of essentially blameless people. Confronted by the daughter of a woman who has killed herself rather than face further humiliation by headline, Robinson snatches for the newsman's standard defence. 'Newspapers', he says, 'are only great mirrors that reflect the world.'

In the 1970s, Hollywood's mirror briefly reflected a more positive image of newsroom life. *All the President's Men* (1976), starring Robert Redford and Dustin Hoffman, told the story of the decade: the *Washington Post*'s exposure of the Watergate conspiracy. Soon, Jane Fonda was exposing nuclear skulduggery in *The China Syndrome* (1979) and Clark Kent, *Daily Planet* reporter turned Superman, made his own transition from comic book to cinema screen. But the sunnier mood didn't last. Films like *Broadcast News* (1987) showed journalistic integrity taking second place to glamour and entertainment, *The Insider* (1998) portrayed television journalism corrupted by corporate self-interest, and in *To Die For* (2000), Nicole Kidman plays a young woman willing to corrupt children and murder her husband in order to get a break in TV news.

Journalism kills

If Hollywood's journalists are ethically challenged, so too in real life. On 15 October 1978, Rupert Murdoch's *News of the World* published a story about a maths teacher, Arnold Lewis, who organized sex parties for consenting adults in his caravan in the Welsh hills. When an undercover reporter phoned Lewis to tell him that the story would soon be splashed across the paper, Lewis gassed himself in his car. At the inquest, the female reporter whose byline appeared on the story was asked by the coroner whether the contents of the dead man's suicide note upset her. 'No, not really,' she replied. Many years later, her editor confessed that the incident still kept him awake at night.

Do journalists take ethics seriously? One of the most widely used text books in the training of British journalists comments that to put these two words in the same sentence 'is to risk reducing the listener to helpless laughter. To the insider on a mass-market tabloid, ethics are largely an irrelevance. Lecturing these journalists about ethics is as pointless as advocating celibacy to sailors arriving in port after six months at sea.' Or, as Kelvin Mackenzie, editor of the *Sun* during the 1980s, once put it: 'Ethics is a place to the east of London where the men wear white socks.'

Piety at the *Post*

There is an aspiration to greater piety elsewhere. The *Washington Post Deskbook on Style* reiterates the principles laid down when Eugene Meyer bought the paper in 1933. It begins: 'The first mission of a newspaper is to tell the truth as nearly as the truth may be ascertained.' Among its other solemn pronouncements is the following: 'The newspaper's duty is to its readers and to the public at large, and not to the private interests of the owner. In the pursuit of truth, the newspaper shall be prepared to make sacrifices of its material fortunes, if such course be necessary for the public good. The newspaper shall not be the ally of any special interest, but shall be fair and free and wholesome in its outlook on public affairs and public men.'

The *Post*'s manual runs to more than 200 pages. Yet, according to one study, the verbosity of such news organization 'bibles' conceals some glaring omissions. Of thirty-three American newspaper manuals analysed by the Poynter Institute in 1999, fewer than one in five codes addressed the subject of editorial and advertising department tensions and many codes ignored the crucial subject of how newspapers do or don't actually enforce their standards, as opposed to proclaiming them.

18. The burglary on the Democratic Party's Watergate offices in 1972 led to the downfall of President Richard Nixon. It also initiated the most famous newspaper investigation of all time and a golden era of investigative reporting. The two reporters, Carl Bernstein and Bob Woodward of the *Washington Post*, were played in the subsequent Hollywood film by Dustin Hoffman and Robert Redford. Since then, every political scandal is labelled 'something-Gate'.

19. The heroic age of journalism, when newspapermen set the world to rights, is nowhere better captured than in the comic-strip stories of Clark Kent, *Daily Planet* reporter, who turns into Superman to combat global evil.

The PCC duvet

In Britain, the BBC's guidelines for producers are also the size of a substantial book, taking in rules on everything from impartiality (which is required by law in the case of all licensed UK broadcasters), fairness, privacy, taste and decency, violence, the depiction of children on television, conflicts of interest, and much else. The *Editor's Code of Practice*, upon which the British Press Complaints Commission bases its adjudication of complaints against newspapers, is a four-page document that gives a good indication of the central ethical standards which journalists in many parts of the world regard as ethically relevant. These are:

- Accuracy, and the prompt correction of inaccuracies.
- The opportunity to reply to attack or criticism.
- Prohibition of invasion of privacy, including by long-lens cameras, except in cases involving genuine public interest.
- Harassment is forbidden, except in cases of public interest.
- Intrusion upon people suffering grief or shock must be 'made with sympathy and discretion'.
- Children should not be bothered at school, or interviewed or photographed without parental consent under the age of 16.
- No use of listening devices, or phone-tapping, except in cases of public interest.
- Hospitals: journalists should not operate covertly.
- Misrepresentation: 'Journalists must not generally seek to obtain information or pictures through misrepresentation or subterfuge.' Such information 'should be removed only with the consent of the owner'. Again, there is a public interest exception.
- An individual's race, gender, religion, sexual orientation, or disability is only to be mentioned in stories where directly relevant.
- Financial journalism: no use for personal profit of information received; no writing about shares in which a journalist has an interest, without permission of the editor.
- Confidentiality of sources must be protected. This is 'a moral obligation'.

- Payment for stories is acceptable, but not where payment is made to criminals or their associates. Again, there is a public interest test.

The self-regulatory approach of the Press Complaints Commission is important, not least because it is based on a very long tradition of press freedom and as such has been much emulated in recent years within emerging democracies in the Balkans, Asia, Africa, and elsewhere. The PCC has also played a key role in developing a global network of self-regulatory press bodies around the Alliance of Independent Press Councils of Europe. These initiatives are not to be confused with the World Association of Press Councils, a body accused by its European enemies of providing a front for state-dominated media organizations, intent upon a censorious global code of ethics for journalists reminiscent of the 'world information order' promoted in the 1980s by UNESCO.

Viewed from this perspective, the PCC is nobly upholding the liberal traditions of the country which pioneered press freedom. How then to explain the contempt in which the PCC is held in some quarters? According to the distinguished journalist and commentator Simon Jenkins, the PCC is 'a somnolent body', which 'emerges sometimes, but only to defend the privacy of Britain's royal families, the Windsors and the Blairs', and which is 'designed largely to keep the newspaper industry out of trouble with politicians, who have in the last two decades repeatedly threatened to legislate to protect citizens against atrocious behaviour by journalists, especially newspaper journalists.'

The case against the PCC is that its rhetoric is strong, but its powers weak. Its only sanction is to oblige newspapers to publish its adjudications and its influence has certainly not prevented newspapers, on a daily basis, declining to make prompt corrections, publishing inaccurate stories, and more or less frequently violating almost every other item in the code. Because so many of its rules may be broken on grounds of 'public interest' (defined as anything which exposes crime, protects public safety, or prevents the public being misled) even those rules which appear strong are in practice negotiable.

So, for example, the rule which forbids payments to criminals or their associates did not prevent the PCC from condoning the *Sun*'s decision in 2001 to pay large sums to the agents and family of Ronnie Biggs, an ageing escaped convict flown back to Britain from Brazil by the newspaper amid great scenes of self-congratulation. When a television newsreader, Anna Ford, protested at the secret photographs taken of her and her children on a foreign beach holiday, her complaint was waved away by the *Daily Mail*, which published the pictures, and by the PCC. Ford branded the PCC 'hopeless', took the matter to court, and lost. At least Ms Ford could consider court action, unlike the un-named asylum seekers accused of eating the Queen's swans – a bogus *Sun* story eventually the subject of a lame apology. These days, it is routine for newspapers to pay for information (a practice once known, disapprovingly as 'cheque-book journalism'), with the result that many stories arise purely from financial motivation, commonly when a young woman, sometimes a professional sex worker, is paid to divulge her account of an evening with some hapless celebrity. To newspapers, celebrities are fair game 'in the public interest'. For such people, employing, say, a nanny has become a high-risk exercise, knowing that the press will always pay large sums for an 'inside story' when the nanny leaves her job. In 2002 the British government announced that it would take steps to outlaw the payment of money by the news media to witnesses in trials. Unsurprisingly, this too provoked a highly questionable expression of outrage at this latest violation of 'press freedom'.

The conclusion of the PCC's sympathetic historian, Richard Shannon, is that its critics will never be satisfied with an organization that can't punish offenders, but that such a regime 'will have to be some arrangement of statutory imposition, which the politicians have made clear they are unwilling to undertake. The result is a comprehensive impasse. Logic is defied, but the system works. It is within the protective embrace of that impasse like a hugely plump duvet, that the PCC survives all hazards, confounds all critics, and lives.'

Self-censorship and other crimes

In the United States, there is no such duvet. Individual newspapers or newspaper groups deal with complaints directly and many have 'readers' editors' or ombudsmen with specific powers to consider complaints and seek correction, right of reply, or other form of adjudication. This practice has, in recent years, started to spread into British newspapers, where some see it as an emerging self-regulatory second tier which will in time enable the PCC to take a tougher stance against serious misbehaviour.

American journalism, however, also faces serious ethical challenges. According to a survey of nearly 300 journalists in 2000, self-censorship in news is commonplace, much of it resulting from journalists bending to pressure from financial sponsors or advertisers – a problem especially acute in local media. More than a third said that 'news which would hurt the financial interests of a new organization goes unreported'. A previous survey, in 1999, showed that journalists increasingly feel that their work is less accurate, that 'the lines have blurred between commentary and reporting', and that 'pressure to make a profit is hurting the quality of coverage'. Half of the journalists questioned thought that their credibility with the public was a major issue. It was to combat this perceived decline in public respect that the Committee of Concerned Journalists came together in 1997, launching its Project for Excellence in Journalism. The project has uncovered data which suggest that only 21 per cent of Americans think the press cares about people, down from 41 per cent fourteen years earlier, and that less than half think the press protects democracy, though this number took a brief upward turn following the events of 11 September 2001. Thirty-eight per cent believed news organizations to be actually 'immoral'.

United they stand

But the same research also discovered that journalists are surprisingly united in their values, especially in their belief that journalism's central purpose is to hold power to account and to provide the resources of information and opinion upon which democracy thrives. 'News professionals at every level . . . express an adamant allegiance to a set of core standards that are striking in their commonality and in their linkage to the public information mission,' concludes one piece of research. On the other hand, the project also confirmed a growing sense of conflict between the goals of the businesses which own the news media and these civic principles. So, although 'every mission statement on file with the American Society of Newspaper Editors names advancing self-government as the primary goal of the news organization,' corporate lawyers 'advised news companies against codifying their principles in writing for fear that they would be used against them in court'. Here is a glaring example of the weakness of a system of professional ethics regulation left to a litigious market place.

A Code from Concern County

Bill Kovach and Tom Rosenstiel, leading figures in the American movement for more traditional standards of journalism, have worked up from this research a set of nine principles which are more general in character than the codifications of the PCC, or broadcaster guidelines, but which seek to identify the characteristics they believe the news media must adopt if they are to be trusted and fulfil their democratic mission. Here is the list in full:

- Journalism's first obligation is to the truth.
- Its first loyalty is to citizens.
- Its essence is a discipline of verification.
- Its practitioners must maintain independence from those they cover.
- It must serve as an independent monitor of power.
- It must provide a forum for public criticism and compromise.

- It must strive to make the significant interesting and relevant.
- It must keep the news comprehensive and proportional.
- Its practitioners must be allowed to exercise their personal conscience.

New news isn't so sure

This, as any first-year media studies student schooled in the subtleties of situational ethics and moral relativism could tell you, is a rather old-fashioned list. Kovach and Rosenstiel acknowledge in their own manifesto that 'the truth' is no longer, if it ever was, uncontested. (A very long time ago, Pontius Pilate asked: 'what is truth?') Critics of the Concerned Journalists have dubbed them barnacle-encrusted defenders of 'Old News', oblivious to the virtues of an emerging 'New News', which is interactive and subject to interrogation, engaging the emotions and the spirit as much as the brain. As long ago as 1992, Jon Katz, the journalist and cultural critic, proclaimed in the pages of *Rolling Stone*: 'something dramatic is evolving, a new culture of information, a hybrid New News – dazzling, adolescent, irresponsible, fearless, frightening and powerful. The New News is a heady concoction, part Hollywood film and TV movie, part pop music and pop art, mixed with popular culture and celebrity magazines, tabloid telecasts, cable and home video.'

'We understand truth as a goal – at best elusive – and still embrace it,' reply Kovach and Rosenstiel. This unalterable goal is, they say, endangered by the 'new' journalism: its speed, the anything-goes spirit of the internet, and the need for journalism to exaggerate in order to stand out. This is 'creating a new journalism of assertion, which is overwhelming the old journalism of verification'. Traditional skills supporting verification, they might have added, such as shorthand and the law, are simultaneously being neglected.

Should journalists be accountable?

To the non-American outsider, the vigour of this debate looks like a promising self-defence mechanism against the complacency of the old journalism and the less desirable aspects of the new. In the United States, wealthy foundations like the Pew Centre for the People and the Press, a backer of the Project for Excellence in Journalism, ensures that there is a quality of data about American journalism which simply does not exist anywhere else, fed by journals like the *Columbia Journalism Review* and the *American Journalism Review*. In Britain, there is a low rumble of assent to some of these ideas, usually without much in the way of comprehensive evidence. 'Print journalism is now the most corrupt realm of life in Britain,' wrote one national newspaper journalist in 2002. 'Some journalists boast of lifestyles that are little more than perpetual junkets – bribes – from those whose news they report.' Or to cite an earlier clarion call, at the launch of the *British Journalism Review*: 'The business is now subject to a contagious outbreak of squalid, banal, lazy and cowardly journalism whose only qualification is that it helps to make newspaper publishers (and some journalists) rich.'

A philosopher intervenes

In recent years, there has been a growing debate outside the journalism profession about these matters. In her Reith lectures of 2002, the philosopher Onora O'Neill took the theme of trust. In her final lecture, she turned to the press which, she said, was guilty of 'smears, sneers and jeers, names, shames and blames. Some reporting covers (or should I say "uncovers") dementing amounts of trivia, some misrepresents, some denigrates, some teeters on the brink of defamation . . . If the media mislead, or if readers cannot assess their reporting, the wells of public discourse and public life are poisoned.'

Onora O'Neill is right that the ethic of truthfulness, or more modestly accuracy, is at the heart of the morality of journalism. Without achieving these, journalism cannot inspire trust and without trust, there is no worthwhile journalism. Industry codes and the law of the land have a part to play in framing and policing the necessary standards, but as we have seen in the financial services industry, which is regulated in minute detail, dishonesty among auditors and senior managers still goes undetected. That is one reason why Kovach and Rosenstiel are also right, in their ninth and final article of faith, to turn to the conscience of the individual journalist.

Working with young, would-be journalists in a journalism school, I encountered real and justified nervousness about the reality of the newsrooms which lay ahead. Is it alright to apply emotional pressure to a parent who has lost a child in tragic circumstances to hand over a treasured picture? Is it OK, as Hildy Johnson suggests, to steal the photo from the mantelpiece? What about stealing a document, or a glance at a document when your interviewee is momentarily distracted, or called from the room? In what circumstances would you lie to get a bigger truth? Would you ever be prepared to disguise or conceal your identity? It depends, doesn't it. It would be acceptable to pose as the purchaser of a dodgy car in order to expose a dealer whose business is in selling dodgy cars. But to pose as a doctor, in order to get someone to tell you their intimate health concerns, would be another matter. Would such intrusion really be justified on the 'public interest' grounds that the subject of the inquiry is famous? In these sorts of cases, code books only get you so far and, in any case, what is forbidden in one news organization may be regarded as a matter for celebration in another. How else to make sense of a professional world which extends from the *Washington Post*'s rule that 'in gathering news, reporters will not misrepresent their identity' to custom and practice on the *News of the World*, whose most famous reporter habitually dresses up as a sheikh in order to entrap his victims? When journalism students ask how they should navigate through a world of such contrasts, it is difficult to make any other reply than this. Journalists are part of the societies in which they work. They acquire, within those societies, a sense of right and wrong; they have, thank goodness, a moral compass learnt outside journalism. It is up to every individual to preserve that compass, to be true to their own and their community's values. In short, don't expect your employer, the news industry or, heaven forbid, your news editor, to do it for you.

Who are these journalists anyway?

If we are to depend, as we must, on journalists and their consciences, supported by quality training and wise guidelines, we also need to know more about journalists, to re-assure ourselves that they are broadly representative of the rest of us. But who are they, these journalists, and in what do they believe?

These questions are not so easily answered as may be imagined since there is no very clear agreement on how to define a journalist. Does the definition include, say, news presenters, who may be actors rather than people trained in news? Does it include radio talk-show and tabloid TV hosts; does it include someone who sets up a weblog on the internet and shares information and opinion with anyone willing to pay attention? What about researchers on a television documentary, or researchers on an entertaining quiz based on the news? Or take the astrology column in a newspaper, which may sit alongside a readers' letters feature: are either of these the work of journalists? Is there a common set of standards to which both might be expected to work?

In Britain, even the number of journalists is subject to a wide range of estimates. Some put the figure as low as 15,000, others as high as 120,000, though the best guess is probably in the 60,000 to 70,000 range. Thanks to a recent, and rare, piece of research, we do at least have a reasonably up-to-date portrait of the British working journalist in the year 2002. The essential characteristics of contemporary British journalists then were:

- as likely to be a woman as a man;
- young: 70 per cent of journalists are under 40;
- childless: only 23 per cent have dependent children;
- white: only 4 per cent are from ethnic minority groups
- metropolitan: 55 per cent work in London and the South East;
- middle-class: only 3 per cent of new entrants have parents who are unskilled or semi-skilled;
- graduates (98 per cent);
- low-paid: the average salary is £22,500, though stars earn more than ten times that level.

The British ethnic minority figure of 4 per cent compares with over 10 per cent of ethnic minority people in the population as a whole, and a proportion much higher than that in the urban centres where most journalists work. In the United States, minorities account for 30 per cent of the population, but fewer than 12 per cent of newspaper journalists.

The global journalist

Professor David Weaver of Indiana University has worked for a number of years with a group of academics around the world, attempting to throw light upon facts about journalists. His research, which covers twenty-one countries, suggests the following:

- Journalism is still a predominantly male occupation, though it is becoming less so. New Zealand and Finland are among the countries that achieved gender balance first.
- Journalists are young, on average in their mid-30s, which is younger than the workforce average.
- They come overwhelmingly and disproportionately from the dominant ethnic group in their societies. This is a serious problem almost everywhere, but especially so in Britain, the United States, Taiwan, and Canada and to a lesser degree in Brazil and China.
- They are increasingly, and in some countries almost universally,

university-educated, though the extent to which they bother with 'journalism schools' or 'journalism degrees' varies.

What do journalists believe?

An even more interesting, and largely unexplored, question is: what do these journalists believe? What is their ethical framework? The researchers found that most journalists agree they are in the business of getting information to the public quickly, but there are wide differences of view about the extent to which journalists see themselves as 'watchdogs' on government or other centres of power. This is a highly rated objective among journalists in Australia, Britain, and Finland, but much less so in countries which lack a long history of democratic government and a culture of a free press. Algeria, Taiwan, and Chile provide examples among the countries surveyed.

Nor could journalists really agree on the importance of their role as analysts, or whether they have an obligation to report accurately or objectively. Only 30 per cent of a British sample agreed that journalists are obliged to be accurate and objective. In Germany, over 80 per cent of journalists, and in the US 49 per cent, accept this obligation. German journalists, who are regarded by their British counterparts as dull and cautious creatures, say they are much less happy about harassing sources, using documents without permission, and paying for information. Impersonation is frowned upon more by journalists in Australia than those of other countries.

It is perhaps not surprising, in the light of findings such as these, that there is confusion about standards of behaviour in journalism. There simply is no lingua franca of journalistic ethics. Journalism is an occupation, especially in newspapers and magazines, which prides itself upon the absence of regulation and which, by its very nature, is simultaneously trying to tune into and challenge the moral and political reflexes of the societies in which it functions. It remains to be seen whether convergence of print and audio-visual media via the internet and other digital platforms will result in regulation of the press becoming more like broadcasting or vice versa. What is certain is that we will not achieve high moral standards in journalism by accident. Journalists, expert at putting others under pressure, need to feel pressure themselves. At the very least, journalists should recognize that we need a well-informed public debate about journalism if journalism is to thrive.

Chapter 8

Matt's modem: tomorrow's journalism

For a couple of years at the end of the 1990s, the world of journalism went crazy. It was impossible to be among journalists without hearing of someone who was leaving their job to set up a web-based news service or an e-zine or to work for Microsoft or Yahoo. There were so many jobs, it became difficult to recruit people into journalism training courses. Who needs training when there are jobs galore for anyone with enthusiasm and a bit of dotcom attitude?

It was a time when everyone thought they needed to be in everyone else's business. Newspapers were terrified that the internet would steal their readers and their classified advertising, so they even started creating websites for advertisers to try to keep them loyal. Magazines rushed to create new identities on-line and in multi-channel television. Television piled into interactive services, to head off the internet challenge. And just about everyone thought about merging to deal with the much proclaimed 'convergence' of digital technologies.

Some gambled billions on these schemes. Others merely doubled the size of their editorial staffs. Newspaper editors wrote of their 'e-epiphanies', as they finally understood that the internet would transform the media. 'What the hell were we all smoking that weekend?' is the question now asked at Time Warner, according to Rupert Murdoch, reflecting upon the decision by Time Warner to sell itself into a merger with America Online at the very peak of dotcom valuations. Never in the history of journalism has a new medium appeared so rapidly out of the blackness and with such volatile consequences. This was journalism on cocaine: the New New Thing meets Woodward and Bernstein. Now the party is over, it remains to figure out what it all means for tomorrow's journalism. How important are these technological issues, against the other concerns discussed in this book, about journalistic ethics, ownership and freedom to publish?

Hacks and hackers

My own experience with the internet began very badly. It was the autumn of 1994 and I was the new editor of the *Independent*, a British daily newspaper born eight years earlier as an independent voice outside the club of traditional newspaper owners. When I took over, the paper was in a mess. Circulation had fallen from a peak of 400,000 to 250,000; Rupert Murdoch had started a price war and the founders had been forced to surrender their independence to a group of large European publishers, who handed management control to the Mirror Group, which was itself still recovering from the aftermath of Maxwell pension-looting scandals.

There was a lot to do. The paper needed redesigning for the *Mirror*'s presses, the editorial budget was slashed, and we moved to offices high in London's biggest office block at Canary Wharf, determined to rebuild sales. We needed to break news, something for which the *Independent* had never been noted. One day, the news editor whispered that we were on to a big story. A young freelancer claimed to have hacked into the computer system of BT, the national telephone company, and gained access to the most secret telephone numbers, including direct lines to defence and intelligence establishments and the prime minister's flat in Downing Street.

It obviously needed a lot of checking. We made enquiries about the reporter, who was in touch with a known network of investigative journalists. He showed us lengthy print-outs of the telephone numbers. We tested them. He said that he had transferred the electronic version of the files to an undisclosed location on the internet. Eventually, we put the allegations to BT, which said its data was secure. We published the story and it caused a stir. The prime minister was asked about it in the House of Commons. A police investigation was launched. We took calls from BT staff contradicting the official BT line: the system was anything but secure, they told us, and this could be proved a second time, if we would make a reporter available.

By now, I was starting to have doubts. A former colleague said the description we had published of the use made by hackers of the internet simply did not ring true. Within a few days, it became clear that the data had been secured not by hackers or gum-shoe journalism, but downloaded from a computer when the reporter worked at BT, on a temporary contract arranged by an employment agency. He had not wished to tell us this, because he thought he would get into trouble. Above all, he wanted to make a name for himself as a journalist.

Meanwhile, another *Independent* reporter was already checking out the calls we had taken from inside BT, appearing to corroborate security lapses. One source offered to prove that our reporter could walk straight past BT's security, sit down at a computer, log on and inspect the secret telephone numbers detailed in our report. This subsequently happened and, as our 'hacker's' story fell apart, we reported the results of the new security breach to our readers. Later our reporter and the BT official were prosecuted, without success, under a new law to protect computer data.

With hindsight, we destroyed a perfectly good story – BT secret data at risk because of slack supervision of contractors – by publishing a bogus one about hacking. The years have intensified rather than diminished my embarrassment because like everyone else I can now see that the way we portrayed the internet in 1994 was deeply ignorant. The idea that the most public medium in the history of communication would be used as a hiding place for a hacker's secret data was a bit like suggesting a gang of bank robbers might choose to hide a sack of stolen bullion on the bar of an East End pub.

The meaning of the internet

So, what do the new digital communications technologies mean for journalism? Some things are clear. Digital offers a huge expansion in the amount of data which can be forced through any communications network, whether wired or wireless, and allows it to be manipulated and displayed upon a range of cheap and simple desk-top, hand-held, or living-room devices. Since the telecommunications network is global, leaving aside issues of investment and communications poverty in large tracts of the world, journalism has become, almost at a stroke, a global enterprise.

For professional journalists, this has very big implications. The global nature of the new communications network means that individuals can consume journalism made all over the world, and discuss it across national boundaries. One result is that the intellectual property rights involved in news are made more valuable. More important, journalism has become a multidirectional force field, rather than the one-way street of the traditional newspaper or television news bulletin. Also, because the technology of news-making and distribution is much cheaper and simpler, almost anyone can join the journalistic mêlée. Today's newsrooms are, essentially, collections of networked personal computers. Today's mobile phones can record and transmit pictures, sound, and text, turning them into primitive television stations. The interplay between mobile phone traffic, live television, and other news media around the 11 September terrorist attacks on America provided a compelling illustration of the way that contemporary political struggles interact with private and public media. When a fever of terrorist bombs caused carnage in London in July 2005, the most dramatic television news pictures were supplied from the mobile phones of travelling Londoners.

It is not, in my opinion, an exaggeration to use the word 'revolution' to describe changes as far-reaching as these, none of which are rendered void by the switch-back motions of the stock market and the valuation of technology, media, and communication stocks. These markets will still play an important role in determining the speed and extent to which truly high-speed broadband communications networks will be rolled out, but nothing the markets can do will turn this revolution around.

What we have already witnessed since the early 1990s is remarkable enough. It is now routine for consumers to receive 200 or 300 television channels, rather than three or four. Radio, rather than being squashed by television, has entered a new and dramatic growth phase, with radio services accessible by computer, digital television, satellite and mobile telephone. Meanwhile, so-called 'pod-casting' has emerged as a technology allowing producers of 'Radio' programmes to share them as digital files with owners of devices like the 'I-pod'. Newspapers, although under pressure for share of advertising markets and reader time, are today able to print at low cost in multiple sites, rather than moving vast quantities of newsprint by road or rail over large distances. They too encounter global possibilities. Magazine titles, supremely well-suited to targeting niches in increasingly fragmented media markets, have also found new opportunities. No medium can target readers across the whole social-demographic spectrum as effectively as magazines.

In television, satellite communications and digital editing make it possible for reporters to transmit stories more or less from anywhere to anywhere, and for editors to process them rapidly for broadcast or internet. Lightweight cameras and other equipment, combined with modern air travel, make it possible for television journalists to be on the scene of stories in hours, where once it would have involved days. To me, it only seems like yesterday that on many foreign assignments the most difficult part of the job was the length of the queue at the local telex station, to transmit a simple text message back to head office. Working as an editor in a national newspaper office, the most irksome aspect of the job up until the 1980s was negotiating with printers. Today, journalists don't even meet printers. News is multimedia, instant, global, and ubiquitous.

Drudge and the kids from *Fame*

As for the internet itself, it has already caused an enormous stir as a medium of news. The medium's patron saint (or, in the eyes of many, patron sinner) is Matt Drudge, the Hollywood-based, one-man-band who started out doing star gossip and movie ratings, but in January 1998 had the American news media at his feet, when he learned that *Newsweek Magazine*, owned by the Washington Post group, had held back from publishing an account of President Clinton's sexual liaison with a White House intern, Monica Lewinsky. Drudge, who had been following the rumours about Clinton's activities for some time, got confirmation of the story from a New York literary agent, wrote his report, and dispatched it to his readers. Although it is very likely that this story would have surfaced without Drudge, the scoop became a point of definition in American journalism, the Watergate of its day, when it precipitated a scramble for follow-ups by established reporters, who cut corners, parading rumour as fact.

It is worth recapturing, in Drudge's own words, the composition of that momentous Drudge Report of 9.02 p.m., Pacific Time, 17 January 1998:

Nothing left to do.

My finger's poised over the button.

This is everything.

Everything you've ever been and everything you'll ever be. . . .

'Whaddya think yer doin', Drudge? . . . '

Cat. Bummer.

'Am I reading this right? You're about to accuse POTUS [the President of the United States] of having it off with an intern? Are you preparing to blow up Washington? Get me Janet Reno . . . !'

Hey, I don't like it either, but it's confirmed confirmed confirmed, and your Janet Reno's authorized Starr to move in. . . .'

'You are a terrorist, aren't you?'

Mommy and Daddy were liberals . . .

'You and your internet manifesto.'

Let the future begin.

'So be it . . .'

Microsoft mouse moved into position.

Ready. Aim. ENTER.

Bouncing beams from dish to dish, e's, faxes & alarms. 1 am
Cellphones, conference calls, dirty dresses, cigars. 2 am
Subpoenas. Grand Juries. Fallout. 3 am.
Elections. Impeachment. 4 am
Acquittal 5 am.
Fame 6 am
Dawn.

Note the penultimate line. Fame: Drudge, the ingénu, knew perfectly well that he was playing for media celebrity. Six months later, he was the guest of the National Press Club in Washington. During his remarks, he spoke idealistically of 'an era vibrating with the din of small voices'. He went on: 'Every citizen can be a reporter, can take on the powers that be. The difference between the internet, television and radio, magazines, newspapers is the two-way communication. The Net gives as much voice to a 13-year-old

20. Matt Drudge, cyber-muck-raker, broke the Monica Lewinsky story on his website. When he faced his professional press critics at Washington's National Press Club, he told them: 'I am not a professional journalist, I am not paid by anyone.'

computer geek like me as to a CEO or Speaker of the House. We all become equal.'

Drudge wears a trilby hat, a conscious reference to 1920s muck-raking journalism, and his supporters see him carrying the torch for the journalistic tradition of Tom Paine. The reaction at the Press Club, however, was not so favourable. Doug Harbrecht, the *Business Week* journalist then serving as Press Club president, led the inquisition, and Drudge scratched hard into his shaky knowledge of American news history to defend himself. But his return fire took casualties. The high-speed, rolling, error-prone editions of on-line journalism he likened to the heyday of the yellow press, when newspapers would turn out a dozen editions a day. If he made mistakes, he said, so did the august news organizations represented in the room. Then he added: 'I put my name on every single thing I write. No "Periscope" here. No "Washington Whispers" there.' Moreover, he said, he was committed to 'cover media people the way they cover politicians . . .

How did a story like Monica Lewinsky break out of a Hollywood apartment? What does that say about the Washington press corps?' The media, he said, 'is comparable to government – probably passes government in raw power', so had to be interrogated. As for the rules of journalism, concerning the number of sources needed to establish a reliable fact before publication, Drudge said: 'I follow my conscience . . . conscience is going to be the only thing between us and the communication in the future, now. And I'm very happy with my conscience.' Recall, if you will, the final, ninth article in the manifesto of 'old journalism', *The Elements of Journalism*: 'practitioners must be allowed to exercise their personal conscience.'

Harbrecht asked whether Drudge foresaw 'a separation of media practices where future journalists accept more your style and methods, or accept the methods of *appropriate* journalism?' Note the menacing, establishment timbre in the word 'appropriate'. The only problem Drudge could see was that, if there were thousands of reporters like him clamouring for attention, 'it could start looking like an insane asylum'. But if that happened, 'I think people will grow disinterested. But again, they'll rally around something else. So I leave this to the free marketplace.' Where, Harbrecht persisted, did this leave the 'professional ethic of journalism'? To which Drudge replied: 'Professional. You see, the thing is you are throwing these words at me that I can't defend, because I am not a professional journalist. I am not paid by anyone.'

By the time you read this book, Matt Drudge may have vanished without a trace, or he may be fronting the most popular talk show on network television. But the issues that his work raises, and the moral hinterland from which he proceeds, are those that have emerged consistently in the themes of this book. The defence of the Western, democratic tradition of newspapers lies in its commitment to free expression and free, competitive markets, even where markets tend to excess. It is a free market that finds space for Thomas Paine, William Randolph Hearst, John Wilkes, Bob

Guccione, the *New York Times*, Michael Moore, and Matt Drudge. It means that the Supreme Court will defend the publishing rights of *Hustler* Magazine, as well as the *Washington Post*. The nobility of principle involved in Thomas Jefferson's according free newspapers a higher democratic priority than free government survives, albeit in high tension with disgust at some of what freedom allows. It should be remembered that, in his later years, Jefferson himself deplored 'the putrid state into which the newspapers have passed and the malignity, the vulgarity and the mendacious spirit of those who write them'. The unmistakable voice of old news and established power, repelled by the outsider.

Bloggers unite

But if the excitements of Drudge's work carry positive reverberations, they do not dispel all doubt about the internet's future. In the press, an earlier era marked by the din of small voices soon gave way to an era of larger, industrial voices, competition for advertising, libel laws, and other civil restraints, which held the worst excesses of newspapers in check, while also in some cases suppressing what ought not to have been suppressed. The press then had to come to terms with competition from the oligopolistic world of broadcast news, which it initially feared would lead to the destruction of newspapers. In practice, television differed from print in terms of the volume and complexity of information each medium could convey and in terms of its relationship with the state. The internet is, in a sense, the bastard child of both broadcasting and print. Some of the biggest players in on-line journalism are television news companies, such as CNN and the BBC. Other news websites are off-shoots of newspapers. But the internet is also home to Matt Drudge and a galaxy of other small-time operators and complete media newcomers, discharging their news, views, and impressions to anyone prepared to pay attention.

Will the internet remain hospitable to such anarchic free-booters? It is difficult to say, but history tells us that no medium of journalism lasts long if it is unsupported by a clear business model and that is where the internet has encountered difficulty. Newspapers, magazines, commercial radio, and most television eventually moved to a model based chiefly upon advertising. But television's diversity has been increased by the availability of subsidy from the taxpayer and today, increasingly, by the emergence of a new revenue stream in subscription-financed channels, programmes, or events. It is interesting to note that the world's highest levels of per capita expenditure on television occur in the United States, which is the largest market, and the United Kingdom, which has in relative terms the largest publicly funded broadcaster.

On-line journalism is still finding its way both financially and creatively. It attracted vast sums of capital in the late 1990s, based largely upon a misunderstanding of the speed with which the internet would transform commercial and personal communication, and has since struggled to build up workable, day-to-day business models. Advertising on the internet is problematic because of the limited size of display screens and the fact that adverts are widely seen as too intrusive in a medium which, unlike television, demands the same level of concentration as reading. But subscription only works for publications with a high 'need to know' element, which is difficult to sustain at a time when news organizations are providing free on-line access to such large amounts of material. Currently, the dominant approach among on-line news services is for the on-line product to draw on the creative resources of the print or broadcast parent, but to offer users additional, paid-for services, such as access to archive.

The advantages of electronic on-line media, however, will continue to assert themselves, as more people have access to on-line information at higher speeds and lower prices. As computing, communications, and screen technologies advance further, it is very likely that we shall see a disposable floppy 'screen', which can be inscribed with electronic 'ink' via a phone line or wireless link, and stuffed into your pocket or briefcase. On-line media have sustainable advantages over print in terms of searchability and interactivity. In time, the business model will settle down.

On-line media also provide a unique opportunity for journalists to combine still and moving pictures, sound, and text. Here lies a great and as yet barely attempted creative challenge, to develop a way of reporting and informing people which feels fresh, startling, and memorable in the way that newspaper publishers did when they first understood how to use headlines, typography, pictures and layout to make navigation of a newspaper more rewarding. Radio made its mark on journalism by bringing the sound of real events to the listener in the Second World War. Television has transfixed us with images of the moment – the young man waving down a tank in Tiananmen Square, the crumbling World Trade Center towers, as well as transforming our relationship with political leaders through the intimacy of the interview.

So far, web journalism has not led to the birth of anything quite so distinctive, apart, perhaps, from the global debating society of chat-rooms and the 'blogosphere'. But as Matt Drudge's work illustrates, the internet has placed the power to shake the mighty in the hands of individuals or small groups: a welcome, if provisional, antidote to media concentration, the hegemony of business values, and the complacency to which all professional groups are prone. The internet has also put into reporters' hands new research tools, sometimes called 'Computer Assisted Reporting', and greatly enhanced the ability of reporters to interrogate public databases, which are slowly becoming more accessible under freedom of information legislation. In purely creative terms too, there are also flares in the night. The work of organizations like the Centre for Digital Storytelling builds upon traditions of oral history and community journalism and puts the tools of multimedia storytelling and journalism into the hands of ordinary citizens. Dana Winslow Atchley, who died in 2000, is a noted pioneer in the digital storytellers' mission 'to thrill those who stand and listen with the notion that they too might have a voice.'

Another recent manifestation of possibility is the web-logging or blogging movement. This, like so much on the internet, was pioneered by an individual and made available to others essentially without charge. It permits anyone to establish a real-time, on-line personal platform, for use as a public diary or pulpit to the world. Andrew Sullivan, a well-known British journalist, and a former editor of the American magazine *New Republic*, describes blogging as 'the first journalistic model that harnesses rather than merely exploits the true democratic nature of the web. It's a new medium finally finding a unique voice. Stay tuned as that voice gets louder and louder.' Sullivan's own weblog raises money through donations and 'affiliate advertising', which means that the blogger gets cash if the site user clicks through to an advertiser and buys something. Sullivan runs a book club, for example, and takes a commission from Amazon, the on-line book retailer, for all books purchased. He comments: 'This means a writer no longer needs a wealthy proprietor to get his message across to readers. He no longer needs an editor, either. It means a vast amount of drivel will find its way to the web. But it also means that a writer is finally free of the centuries-old need to suck up to various entities to get an audience. The universe of permissible opinions will expand. It's no accident that a good plurality of American bloggers are libertarian or right of centre. With a couple of exceptions the established newspaper market in America is dominated by left-liberal editors and reporters. What the web has done is allow talented writers to bypass this coterie and write directly to an audience. If the Drudge Report pioneered the first revolution of this kind, then bloggers are the vanguard of the second wave.'

Life and death

Activities such as blogging and digital storytelling will acquire even greater potential, as higher speed communications networks take shape. There is good reason to hope that these might also help fill the growing gaps in local and community news services, which have opened up as largely monopoly newspapers have cut their reporting resources and relaxed in the absence of competition. Multimedia on-line communication is also an essential feature of other news networks, such as those formed by fans in sport and entertainment, as well as in specialized fields like science and the law. No professional communicator should doubt the power of the internet in the hands of the curious and determined citizen, as poignantly illustrated in the case of 'Miss B', a 43-year-old British woman who demanded of her doctors that they turn off her life support machinery a year after she was paralysed in an accident. The case was heard by a judge at the bedside of Miss B, who explained that her trust in her doctors had been undermined when she surfed the internet and found 'a tremendous amount of information, not just from professionals, but also from other quadriplegics, who are also ventilated'. Empowered by this information, Miss B made her case and won from the court permission to die, the first recorded case of internet-euthenasia.

The vibrating din of small voices also enables other professional communicators, such as public relations experts, to communicate directly with the public, rather than only through the media. At the same time, the public relations people must contend with the fact that new media also allow individuals and groups to mount significant media campaigns against much larger opponents. In the 1990s, anyone who searched the internet for the restaurant company McDonalds quickly found themselves routed to sites run by McDonalds' many angry critics. At the same time, so-called 'independent media centres' have sprung up around the world on the back of demonstrations challenging the values of global capitalism and to provide alternative dimensions of reporting around major events such as the Iraq War. These centres see themselves as reporters unsullied by the preoccupations of the mainstream media. The response of the public relations industry has been to invest heavily in web monitoring, in order to maintain a real-time watch on chat rooms and other internet-based communications forums, before using 'viral' techniques for rebuttal and response.

Aux armes citoyens! plurality, diversity, and trust!

Just how this competition between a din of small voices and the ever-growing scale of the biggest media companies will shake down is difficult to judge. Those who feel pessimistic about the corporatization of the internet and the predicted loss of its diversity should perhaps take comfort from the difficulties now being endured by the new giants: AOL–Time Warner, Disney, and Vivendi. Equally, those inclined to optimism should recall that power, in the end, follows money in the media, which is why, even in a media world much more difficult to regulate than previously, there will still be good grounds for taxpayers to invest constructively in public service television and radio and for deploying strong powers to prevent excessive concentrations of media ownership. A new challenge will be to ensure that access to communications infrastructures is affordable and fair, in rural as well as urban areas, in poor countries as well as richer ones. Without this, there will be a 'digital divide' which will undermine democracy. If the slogan of the French revolutionaries was 'liberty, equality, and fraternity', the slogan of the ongoing communications revolution should be: 'access, plurality, diversity, and trust'.

The confusion of the times arises from the fact that so many apparently contrary things are happening at the same time: we have blogging and AOL–Time Warner; independent media centres and the rise of the global public relations firm; Matt Drudge and the $50m TV news presenter. To some extent, these phenomena can be explained as reactions to each other, all part of the restless churning of the news media, as they resist confinement by old technologies, old establishments, and old certainties.

Gutenberg galaxy to internet galaxy

According to Manuel Castells, whose great trilogy of books in the 1990s mapped the 'network society,' the unique culture of the internet will preserve it from take-over by corporations or emasculation by governments, so long as the net's governance is not dominated by American interests. The internet, says Castells, is 'a particularly malleable technology, susceptible of being deeply modifed by its social practice, and leading to a whole range of potential social outcomes – to be discovered by experience, not proclaimed beforehand. . . . it is the expression of ourselves.'

Castells has suggested that 'if convergence takes place one day, it will be when the investment required in setting up broadband capabilities beyond the instrumental uses of the corporate world is justified by a new media system willing and ready to satisfy the most important latent demand: the demand for interactive free expression and autonomous creation – nowadays largely stymied by the sclerotic vision of the traditional media industry.' Journalism is self-evidently only an aspect of this larger creative picture, yet there is no denying that it will both shape and be shaped by the forces Castells identifies. The combination of social, political, technological, cultural and economic circumstances which gave us the liberal free press settlement in the eighteenth century no longer exists in the same form today. As we navigate our way from McLuhan's 'Gutenberg Galaxy' to Castells' 'Internet Galaxy', the driving force is the citizen-consumer, who today demands maximum choice and maximum quality; the benefits of well-functioning markets and protection from their shortcomings and excesses. When it comes to news, the mood of the citizen-consumer is fickle, flitting from one medium to another and picking up news at his or her convenience rather than feeling obliged to track some fixed canon of 'the news'.

The internet is both a news medium in its own right and a

connector of other media. It facilitates global shopping, as well as global journalism. Although the *Washington Post*'s Leonard Downie and Robert Kaiser, voices of 'old news', are snootily dismissive of the achievements of on-line journalism, and 'new news' generally, they are honest enough to note that 'in 2001, Drudge sent more readers to washingtonpost.com than did any other web site that linked to the Post.' Tom Rosenstiel, a founder of the Committee of Concerned Journalists, and another campaigner for 'old news' values, goes further and agrees that 'ultimately, journalism will probably be saved by the advent of the new technologies because they create the capacity for ten young people in a garage to invent a journalism that flows out of the needs of the people they know, the communities they want to serve, rather than some sophisticated model from business consultants about how to maximise profitability. The first journalism in the 1600s was literally conversation among citizens in coffee houses in England. The internet is our new coffee house.'

The age of the virus

Advocates of public journalism are right to remind us that journalism is both a business and much more than a business. As the writer on media issues Christopher Dornan has said: 'Who could have imagined that the media would come to usurp political authority, buffering the policy process and decision-makers in the chaotic turbulence of perception? In the United States of America, the most advanced and sophisticated nation on the planet, what matters now is not so much what is done, but how actions play out in the mediascape. Journalism was supposed to provide reliable records of the real. Now, it seems, a stew of journalism, entertainment and infotainment establishes what is taken to be real – not as the Chomskyites insist, according to some master plan for the manipulation of the masses, but in absurd, directionless and irrational gyrations. What Huxley and Orwell feared was the dominance of collective order over the individual. What we have arrived at is something close to the end of governance as it was once defined. When the media run the show, then the jabber and the images of the airwaves take precedence over what the images were originally meant to depict, no one is in charge.' In Orwell's Room 101, Dornan adds, the authoritarian tormentor creates 'a world in which the very concept of trust has been exterminated'. But trust can be as readily lost in a mist of infotainment as in the snows of a Stalinist terror.

The first job of journalism is to find out, communicate accurately, and be trusted. If it cannot be trusted, then it will be neither believed nor respected. To a large extent, market mechanisms operating within a framework of strong competition policy will do the job of sorting out the trustworthy from the unreliable, but well-functioning markets also need honest, accountable suppliers, ready to correct mistakes and willing to submit to public scrutiny and debate. There is a role here for intelligent regulation and journalists would be wise to welcome it. As Onora O'Neill said in her attack upon contemporary journalism, if the news media are to be part of the solution, not part of the problem for democracy, they must provide 'reporting we can assess and check', which means that free news media must collaborate with effective regulatory mechanisms to illuminate their conflicts of interest and admit their errors. Well-run markets can deliver plurality and diversity of news provision, but trust requires something more from everyone involved in public communication: politicians, campaigners, and businesses, as well as journalists. If the politicians and business people are lying, the journalists will be thanked for saying so. If the journalists are lying, or failing to find out, there is no possibility that the public sphere will be in good health.

The danger is that the time-constrained citizen finds the whole debate encompassed in these pages too wearisome and too remote. Then, they will note the unreliability of much news and switch off, settling for a quieter life, away from the information storm. This is the great peril, the way free societies might indeed perish; lost in media space, with no direction home. Democracy needed

21. The dotcom boom and bust came and went so fast that those reporting the story could barely keep up. This cover of a British internet magazine is dated August 2000. By February 2001, the cover of the American magazine Fast Company indicates the extent to which the mood has changed.

journalism to get started. Journalism needs to re-absorb the values of democracy into its own self-conduct if it is to function effectively: to open itself to scrutiny and challenge.

There is a Chinese proverb about the dangers of failed leadership: that the fish rots from the head. In complex modern democracies, this is not so. We are living in the age of the network and the age of the virus, which can strike anywhere and spread in any direction. In that sense, modern democracies are less vulnerable and more stable than those which appear to be in the grip of elites. On the other hand, once a virus gets moving, pretty soon it is everywhere and the problem cannot be solved by a change in leadership. Against such viruses, reliable, accurate, truthful journalism is the only known antidote. Where the market can't deliver it, we must continue to ensure that market failure is corrected.

By the way, when Doug Harbrecht asked Matt Drudge to name *his* greatest mistake, he replied: 'ever doubting my ability'.

Further reading

Michael Bromley and Tom O'Malley (eds.), *A Journalism Reader* (London: Routledge, 1997) contains many landmark documents, including W. T. Stead's vision of 'government by journalism'.

Manual Castells, *The Internet Galaxy* (Oxford: Oxford University Press, 2001).

Benjamin Compaine and Douglas Gomery, *Who Owns the Media?: Competition and Concentration in the Mass Media Industry* (Mahwah, NI: Lawrence Erlbaum, 2000).

James Curran and Jean Seaton, *Power Without Responsibility: The Press and Broadcasting in Britain* (London: Routledge, 1997).

Leonard Downie and Robert Kaiser, *The News about the News: American Journalism in Peril* (New York: Alfred A. Knopf, 2002)—gloomy analysis from *The Washington Post*.

Mohammed El-Nawawy and Adel Iskandar, *Al-Jazeera: How the Free Arab News Network Scooped the World and Changed the Middle East* (Cambridge, MA: Westview Press, 2002).

Stephen Glover (ed.), *Secrets of the Press* (London: Penguin, 1999) includes good essays by Paul Foot and others.

Ian Hargreaves and James Thomas, *New News, Old News* (London: Independent Television Commission, 2002)—research since developed in other work, available at *www.ofcom.org*.

John Hartley, *Popular Reality: Journalism, Modernity, Popular Culture* (London: Arnold, 1996).

John Keane, *The Media and Democracy* (London: Polity Press, 1991).

Philip Knightley, *The First Casualty: The War Correspondent as Hero and Myth-Maker* (London: Prion, 2001) is a classic on this subject.

Bill Kovach and Tom Rosenstiel, *The Elements of Journalism: What Newspapers Should Know and the Public Should Expect* (New York: Crown Publishing, 2001)—this is the manifesto of America's 'concerned journalists'.

Howard Kurtz, *The Fortune Tellers: Inside Wall Street's Game of Money, Media and Manipulation* (New York: Touchstone, 2001).

Larry Langman, *The Media in the Movies: A Catalogue of American Journalism Films 1900–1996* (Jefferson, NC: McFarland, 1998).

Walter Lippmann (ed.), *The Washington Post Desk Book on Style* (New York: McGraw-Hill, 1989).

John Lloyd, *What the Media Are Doing to Our Politics* (London: Constable and Robinson, 2004) takes the politicians' side against declining standards of news media behaviour.

Janet Malcolm, *The Journalist and the Murderer* (New York: Alfred A. Knopf, 1990).

John Stuart Mill, 'On Liberty', in *Utilitarianism*, ed. Geraint Williams (London: Everyman, 1972).

Onora O'Neill, *A Question of Trust*: The BBC Reith Lectures (Cambridge: Cambridge University Press, 2002).

George Orwell, *Essays* (London: Penguin, 2000)—exemplary journalism.

The Pew Center for People and the Press, website *www.people-press.org*, is the best American database and discussion zone on issues of news media standards.

John Pilger, *Hidden Agendas* (London: Vintage, 1998) presents a view of the issues from the Left.

Richard Shannon, *A Press Free and Responsible* (London: John Murray, 2001) is a fairly official history of the Press Complaints Commission.

Bill Sloan, *I Watched a Wild Hog Eat My Baby! A Colorful History of Tabloids and their Impact* (New York: Prometheus, 2001).

Tom Wolfe, *The Purple Decades* (London: Jonathan Cape, 1983)—or any other compendium from the master of the late-20th-century version of 'the new journalism'.

For inspiration in digital story-telling, go to *www.storycenter.org*, *nextexit.com* or *photobus.co.uk*.

Index

Expand your collection of
VERY SHORT INTRODUCTIONS